YOUR BRAIN
GOES TO CHURCH

YOUR BRAIN GOES TO CHURCH

Neuroscience and Congregational Life

BOB SITZE

The Alban Institute
Herndon, Virginia
www.alban.org

The Alban Institute, 2121 Cooperative Way, Suite 100, Herndon, VA 20171

Scripture quotations, unless otherwise noted, are from the New Revised Standard Version of the Bible, copyright © 1989, Division of Christian Education of the National Council of the Churches of Christ in the United States of American and are used by permission.

Cover design by Mary Byrd Productions
Text design by The HK Scriptorium

Library of Congress Cataloging-in-Publication Data

Sitze, Bob.
   Your brain goes to church : neuroscience and congregational life / Bob Sitze.
      p. cm.
   Includes bibliographical references and index.
   ISBN 1-56699-299-0
   1. Pastoral psychology. 2. Brain—Religious aspects—Christianity. I. Title.

BV4012.S53 2004
253.5'2—dc22
                 2004023844

09   08   07   06   05   VG   1   2   3   4   5   6   7   8   9   10

For Bob Sylwester,
whose brain has accompanied me
to church and beyond

Contents

Foreword

THE GOLDEN AGE of biology began in 1953, with the discovery of DNA, biology's regulatory mechanism. Dramatic advances in computer technology during the last quarter of the twentieth century added an unprecedented direct access to the awesome complexity but elegant simplicity of organisms—and so we entered the twenty-first century with a wondrous cascade of remarkable advances in genetics and the brain sciences.

The initial focus of all this biological research was on the solution of medical problems, but researchers are now advancing our understanding of the neurobiology of teaching and learning, of market and political persuasion, of personal and social identity—and even of religious experience. Very much of what we now know about our brain and cognition has only emerged during the past few years.

The literature of science is dynamic, continually changing as new discoveries replace current knowledge. The basic literature of Christian theology is static—requiring that new discoveries be incorporated into Scriptures written thousands of years ago. One result of this difference is that although the Bible describes many medical problems, it offers no remedy for them beyond compassion. Conversely, the dynamic nature of science has allowed it to use new biological discoveries to develop successful remedies.

This poses the issue of the current relevance of an unchanging theological base in a rapidly changing, increasingly scientific and technological world. Uncertainties and incongruities abound. Parishioners accept PowerPoint sermons, but expect the sermon content to focus on enduring values. The church is not of one mind on many moral issues related to scientific discovery. Guitars and drums can occasionally but not permanently replace the pipe organ. Caffe lattes are okay during the week, but regular perked coffee is more appropriate between Sunday services.

Why would a society that eagerly embraces scientific and technological developments that are often antithetic to theology continue to also embrace the religious life? Indeed, the most robust recent growth has occurred within Christianity's evangelical community, the most dubious of science and technology. Scientists wonder, for example, why folks who reject Darwinian principles of biology use medications that emerged out of those theories, seemingly unconcerned about the inconsistency between their beliefs and behavior.

Perhaps it's because many people perceive a clear separation between science and theology. Science is good at solving the *how* problems (how to understand or do something) but not so good at the *should* problems (should I do it), and the reverse is true of theology. Theology emerged millennia ago, when much of the physical world was viewed as mystical, and only limited technologies existed for understanding it. So theology was useful for providing advice on how people should live, based principally on extended observations of folks who did and did not do very well at it. These observations were codified into a biblical format that was passed on from generation to generation. The strength of the Bible is thus in its human scale—in that an incomprehensible world and God were translated into a marvelous comprehensible and frequently metaphoric human-scale narrative.

Science arrived within the last several centuries to make an incomprehensible world comprehensible. It was initially dominated by the powerful moral or ethical judgments of theology. Indeed, many scientists were also theologians (for example, Gregor Mendel, geneticist, was a monk, and Charles Darwin, biologist, had planned to be a theologian). Over time, however, science became less concerned about the morality and more concerned about the objective validity of its discoveries. Ideally the two disciplines would have made a great tag team, but theologians were fearful of this new upstart. Some scientific discoveries seemingly contradicted biblical accounts—and so theology regrettably built a heretical wall rather than a conversational bridge between the two. This book is about the current need to make a door in that wall.

Bob Sitze approaches his task through a marvelous biological property: a few elegantly simple biological processes are repeated throughout the biosphere—within cells, organs, organisms, and societies. So if you understand how one level functions, you can understand how all levels function.

For example, we have turned a few dozen meaningless phonemes (and letters) into a meaningful language of 500,000 words by adapting the particle principle that constructs chemical compounds and proteins. The principle is that a relatively small number of stable particles— atoms, amino acids, or phonemes—can be hierarchically assembled into an infinite number of complex combinations. Thus, only 20 different amino acids and 44 different phonemes can be assembled into myriads of proteins and words because the information in proteins and words is not coded into the amino acids and phonemes themselves, but rather into the DNA sequence of amino acids that constitutes a gene (that assembles a protein), and the sound sequence of phonemes that constitutes a word (such as do, dog, god, good, goods).

We thus provide our children with a sequential genetic language at conception that tells them how to assemble their body, and a similarly organized verbal language after birth to tell them how to live as a human being. This simple biological principle thus beautifully expands the biblical statement, "In the beginning was the word"—the deoxyribonucleic acid (DNA) *word* and the biblical *word*. A great team!

This book appropriately argues that religious belief and thought are centered in our brain—and that a parish is made up of a society of somewhat similar brains. To understand the biology and psychology of a brain thus helps us to understand the sociology and theology of a parish—and the neurosciences are now providing us with an unprecedented understanding of our brain's organization, maturation, and operation. So it's two for one time—you'll learn intriguing things about both your brain and your parish through this book.

A strength of this book is that it does not presume to provide answers, but rather that it takes you and your fellow parishioners on an imaginative exploratory tour of what is occurring within your individual skulls and your collective church building. The scientific terminology may occasionally bog you down, but then ecclesiastical terminology also bogs us down. Check unfamiliar brain terms in the glossary—and realize that brain and theological terms are not as important as their functions. The brain facts are just there to continually remind you that a brain, much like a parish, is a real living biological entity.

The book will focus on several sets of biological concepts that are central to understanding both a brain and a parish—belief and knowledge, growth and development, foreground and background, danger and opportunity, learning and memory—all of which combine to regulate movement, the central property of our brain and of the Christian church. We move from here to there, and from sin to grace.

I enjoyed reading the manuscript. I occasionally hassled Bob about his science and theology during the book's development—but that's okay because both science and theology spark social interaction. We now know a lot more about both than we used to, but we do not know as much as we think we know. But we're all sure that we're correct—orthodoxy is my kind of doxy and heterodoxy is your kind of doxy. It is certainly not yet time for a definitive catechism about the proper relationship between twenty-first century biology and timeless theology.

So the nice thing is that you and your friends get to explore the integration of science and theology through this book—and that is much more stimulating than merely memorizing what others have decided. Read the book in that spirit of free exploration. And then explore.

Robert Sylwester
Emeritus Professor of Education
University of Oregon

Preface

"YOUR BRAIN GOES TO CHURCH." Clever title, hmm? At least clever enough to catch your eye and engage the brain cells that help your hands pry open books. Inventive enough to set your brain a-wondering. Imaginative enough to light up the sections of your brain that like to play with "new."

Now that you've opened the cover, you may be wondering what you're getting into. This book combines brain science with the sociology of religion. That odd mixture may make this stuff hard to explain and read—like trying to eat broccoli and raspberry ice cream together. You may have to think over some parts of the book more than once. That's okay.

As you read this book you're going to be intrigued, excited, and confused—probably all at once. You may feel like a dog in a butcher shop trying to sort out all those emotions, all these facts and possibilities. This is normal. It's happened to all of us who started thinking about "brains and the church," however long ago we started. Because brain science is changing so fast, some of us are still trying to sort out all the information and possibilities years after we first encountered

> **Brain Fact**
>
> Some brain structures go by different names. For example, *forebrain, cerebrum, hemispheres, neo-cortex,* and *cerebral cortex* are all names for the same region of the brain.

the subject. Because brain and theological terminology can be confusing—interrelated ideas or structures sometimes have several different names—some of us are still trying to figure out who's on first, and what team's at bat. You might want to put a bookmark in the glossary of this book to help you with the terms.

A Simple Proposition

Applied brain science explains many of the features or facets of your congregation in practical ways. Some of what you learn from brain science might make you want to stop, curtail, or avoid what you're doing in your congregation. That's when "simple" might get difficult.

I think this book will be worth your time. Not because I wrote it, but because applied brain science may be like an uncharted galactic frontier for ecclesiology. This may be a chance for you to visit one edge of an as-yet-unknown universe! It's the right time to think about the universe of brain science. This field of human inquiry is growing fast. Its deeper theories are moving into metaphysics, a second cousin to theology. Business, education, government—all of these human enterprises are trying to carve "useful" out of "interesting" and "informative." It's time the church did the same.

Because the work of applying brain science to congregational dynamics is only just beginning, this book is full of questions, both explicit and implied. As an activity of the brain, question-making is a complex behavior. When you and I form and ask questions, they're the result of basic brain functions such as curious musings, straight-forward puzzlements, hesitant mappings of what's only partially known, and the forming of relationships and statements that allay fear. Question-construction makes use of a significant number of brain functions that help us construct and organize meaning.

Brain Fact

Hypergraphia (high-pehr-GRAFF-ee-uh) is the name of a strong, brain-based drive to write a great deal of words, of whatever quality, for the sheer pleasure of writing. Hypergraphics write about themes they believe to be important, mostly philosophical, autobiographical, or religious.

Throughout this book, my questions are usually followed by question marks, but sometimes I'll express them as statements loaded with qualifiers—look for "may," "seem," "could be," and "might be."

To answer your questions, I'll try to imagine the complex curiosities from which your questions might arise. I'll respect your intelligence and I'll try to think of your viewpoint as a congregational leader. One thing I won't do is think of questions as the iceberg-tips of dangerous knowledge. Although some faithful Christians may think of brain science as a kind of apostasy, I don't feel that way about this part of God's revelation in the world. My experience over almost three decades is exactly the opposite. When questions about the brain are not asked, what becomes "dangerous" (and fearsome) is the lack of knowledge! Think how many cultish religious leaders have captured the minds of their unwitting devotees and advocated mindless "discipleship" as the accepted norm for Christian living.

I am aware that the matters we'll look at together in this book may jar some of your beliefs and challenge some of your present knowledge. I understand how brain science might seem to threaten the things you hold most dear about the church or your ministry. And I respect your possible concern that brain science may lead the church into new or old heresies and idolatries. That being said, however, I invite you to approach this book's application of neuroscience with a mind open to new possibilities.

Big Question

Throughout the book you'll find places where I've inserted a "big question." What makes a question big? How it draws together the subjects of the chapter into a collective question that won't be soothed or solved by quick answers. Another way to gauge the supposed size of a question is to determine how many little questions spin off of it.

To prepare yourself for this book's propositions and invitations, revisit how you actually feel about being a leader in your congregation. To identify and sort those feelings, try asking yourself the following questions:

- Have you wondered why current theories and practices about congregations don't fit your situation as well as you've hoped?
- Do your spiritual churnings continue, no matter how hard you try to calm them?

- Are you still dissatisfied with the way your congregation's vision or mission statements answer questions about what your congregation is really about, and about what kind of leader you're supposed to be?
- How easily do you welcome strange facts and concepts?
- How do you react to ideas that don't light up easily?
- Where do you find the patience and the energy to try "What if?" questions whose answers might lead in new directions? ("What if this congregation operated more like an employee-owned enterprise?")
- How have you resisted the temptation to check your brain at the door to the church? (Ironically, in some places overly compliant followers, who agree mindlessly to do what they're told, are rewarded for that behavior by being named "leaders.")

Trying It Out

Throughout the book, I'll offer specific invitations for you and others to put into practice some of what you read here. I'll feed you ideas for tasks or give you assignments to carry out, ways for you to enrich the ideas in this book with experiences you gather in your own setting. Look for "Trying It Out" boxes.

If you're still wrestling with questions like these, you're probably already equipped to handle what you read here. You're ready to lay a new map—brain science—over the familiar territory of what's happening in your congregation. You're prepared to find new names for well-known facets of your congregation's life. You're set for surprises, delightful ideas, and imaginative musings!

You're ready to read this book; that means you're curious—about your brain and about your congregation. I want to honor that attitude in two ways. I hope both are helpful:

1. I'll tell you what I've discovered and what I think after almost thirty years of reading in brain science and applying what I read to the workings of congregations.
2. I'll ask questions and think about possibilities so that we can both see how brain science and ecclesiology work together to help us

understand congregations. Perhaps your curiosity will find its voice in mine.

I respect your searching alongside of me. Because it's new ground for both of us, this may not be an easy task. Because I think of you as someone I'd like to meet sometime, we'll do this work together. We'll be signs of God's grace for each other...and our brains will go to church together.

Acknowledgments

THIS BOOK WAS WRITTEN with the help of a village of prized friends, colleagues, and helpful scholars who offered their wisdom and expertise, adding substance to the words you will soon read. Each of these helpful souls shares my belief that brain science is a valuable tool by which to shape congregations. They gave me courage. They shaped my words and my brain. Without them, this book would have not gone to church.

Carol Rausch Albright, for early encouragement and assurance about "who has the right to write any book," and for the connections to philosophy and complexity theory.

Jay Beech, musician, composer, wry ecclesiastical observer, and humorist, for not getting involved with this project in any way, thus freeing me for a more serious and scholarly approach to writing.

Beth Gaede, wordsmith and word sculptor, editor and friend, for being the grace-filled and eternally insistent muse for this book.

Sally Simmel, for all the enthusiastic hints and helps, readings and clippings, offered over all the years this book was hatching.

The Stewardship Team of the Evangelical Lutheran Church in America (Laurel Hensel, Nancy Snell, Michael Meier, Marcie Rogers, Nancy Oakford, Kathy Hetland), with thanks for their patient listening to these ideas over all these years, and for incorporating brain science into their vocabularies and work when I wasn't looking.

Phil Hefner, for showing me other places to explore in the universe of brain science.

Bob Sylwester, brain-based educator, writer and metaphor-maker, for the initial spark of interest in neuroscience, first lit in 1978 and still burning. For mentoring and advising, encouraging and feeding the flame when I thought it had gone out. For the chapter-framing metaphors that capture galaxies of information and make them sparkling spots of light that readers can hold in their hands. More than anything else, I thank Bob for his unflagging determination that my brain science facts remain up-to-date and that my words soar past prosaic.

Carolyn Heider, for being the first respectful skeptic who forced my wild-eyed ideas into defensible legitimacy.

Superb conversationalists and ELCA colleagues Jonathan Reitz, Lita Brusick Johnson, Phil Reitz, Rod Boriack, Anne Basye, Sue Engh, Bill Kees, Heidi Hagstrom, and Ted Schroeder, for their probing questions and wide-ranging curiosity about this passion.

Chris Sitze, brain-savvy elementary school teacher and coconspirator in this part of our shared life work, for sticking with me through all the self-doubts and false starts on this project, and for being soulmate all these years.

Introduction

What's a Nice Brain Like You Doing in a Place Like This?

THE PAGES OF THIS BOOK are filled with ideas about how the inner workings of your brain connect with the inner workings of your congregation—how what's inside of your head makes church possible, even when most people don't seem aware of it—and how church makes what's inside of your head possible. Beneath all of the brain science and ecclesiology, this book is about God's creating and sustaining you as a leader in the church. Maybe even about how you're going to change some of the ways you think and act in your congregation.

This Is Astounding Stuff

The word *astound* has an interesting root meaning. It comes from the Latin word *extonare,* which means "to strike with thunder." Along the way to Modern English, the French and Anglo-Saxon derivatives of *extonare* picked up the idea that "sudden wonder" is whole, complete, and mind-filling.

"Sudden wonder" is what may happen to you as you read about brain science. No loud claps of thunder, perhaps, but a thundering inside your brain that says, "Yes! This explains such-and-such!" or "Now I know why...!" I hope you experience "aha!" moments as you consider what the facts and theories of brain science might mean for your life and for your congregation.

1

Anticipation is an example. Your brain lives in a state of anticipation, ready for a range of possibilities that are determined by its experience over time. Anticipation is a way of describing the constant firing of neurons in what could otherwise seem like just random activity. Another way of saying this is that except in genuinely surprising situations, your brain is keeping itself ready for what comes next. Even when they're resting, your brain's circuits—or bundles of neurons—are preorganized for action. This means that you can react quickly—or automatically—to almost every situation you face. Anticipation is a filter that keeps you focused, filtering out what doesn't need to be attended to.

Astounding, isn't it? Your brain isn't a merely reactive organ, waiting like a knee to jerk into place once the right stimulus comes along. At the level of its individual cells, your brain is always making decisions. Taken to the level of your whole person, this means that you're not a reactive victim. Rather, you are always ready to take action, because deep down you know what to do.

How might this idea apply to the workings of your congregation-as-brain?

- Like the single cells of your brain, each individual member of your congregation probably knows what to do in most situations, and is ready to take action.
- Like bundles of cells—or an entire brain—your congregation has the capability to be more than just the reactive victim of its circumstances.

Hear any thunder yet? Ready to find some sudden wonder?

The Brain's Where It Starts

Although the language of the church still honors ancient ways of explaining where the body is centered—"heart" or "bowels," for example—all matters of faith occur within the limits and mysteries of the human brain. You know God in your brain, not in your heart. Your feelings of mercy are not located in your lower intestinal tract, but probably occur within several interrelated areas of your brain, where natural self-ishness is thwarted or overridden by other-mindedness. Your feelings of mystical unity with God and with all of God's people are similar to the feelings those with epilepsy experience during seizures. When you meditate deeply, activity in a brain structure called the posterior superior parietal (pah-RYE-ih-tuhl) lobe quiets down—the decrease of blood and electro-chemical energy can be seen on the screens of brain-imaging machines. However it might be described theologically, the soul is most likely a feature of your brain, perhaps its control or pleasure centers, or its collective self-awareness.

Brain Fact

Up until the early 1800s, common belief held that the heart was the human organ responsible for the workings of the body. The first notable scientist to suggest otherwise was Franz Joseph Gall, who proposed that the bumps on one's skull showed where in the brain certain functions took place. He called it *phrenology,* from the Greek word for *mind.* Fortunately, this pseudo-science—replete with maps and fanciful descriptions—was only a passing fad.

The Brain's *Not* Where It Starts

Matters of faith and congregational life cannot be reduced, however, to mechanistic notions of simple chemistry, physics, and biology. To twist the metaphor, matters of the brain have to include the heart.

In this book I'll take the view that God created the brain, and not vice versa. However it happened, and whenever it happened, God's powerful *fiat* brought the human brain into being. Because of the shaping influences of genes and environment this organ of the human body was given mental capacities that transcend those of the rest of God's created living things. Simply put: no God, no brain. Another way to look at it: know God, know brain.

In these pages I'll write from the position that God's action is pre-eminent and causal. God fashions and shapes the brain through God's original and continuing creation. God's wisdom is given to the human brain before birth and through the vagaries of life's experiences. God's favor and grace overwhelm the brain's misanthropic attempts to wallow in selfish individualism.

The church—and all the brains that comprise it—begins with God as well. The church is not simply explained as the result of evolutionary herd instincts in the brains of humans. Its effectiveness—and ineffectiveness—are not primarily defined by brain-based sociology. Instead, as Martin Luther explains it, God's Spirit "calls, gathers, enlightens and sanctifies the whole Christian church on earth, and keeps it with Jesus Christ in the one, true faith" (from the Explanation of the Third Article of the Apostles' Creed). Like the human brain, the church is created and sustained by God's action. Ministry of Word and Sacrament, loving care and selfless service are all gifts of God's Spirit.

Your Brain Goes Everywhere in the Church

By now you should have caught another major premise of this book: every moment of the church's life, every facet of its behavior, every doctrine or practice, and every fervent purpose is dependent on some action of the human brain. When your brain goes to church, it both creates and

?

Big Question

In life, where you end up depends on where you start, and where you start depends on where you want to end up. What problems or opportunities do you see starting or ending important inquiries with brain science? What problems or opportunities do you see starting or ending the same life questions with theology?

reacts to every single element of the church's good and godly activity. There is nothing in the life of the church that is not perceived, affected, or actionable by the brains of those who constitute the church.

"Your brain goes to church" also characterizes how functional arrangements that run through all of creation also run through the church. This means that in profound and simple ways the structures and functions of the brain can be seen in the structures and functions of individual human beings *and* of congregations.

For example, take the simple and complex progression of input–process–output. At the single cell level, this phrase describes how the dendrites on a neuron bring chemical information to a cell body. The cell body processes the information and then sends out an electrical-chemical signal to other neurons. Those neurons, in turn, can either continue or stop the action. The same activity characterizes your interaction with the environment and with other people, as you take in information, process it, and then decide whether to take or refrain from action. The entire congregation gathered for worship receives the wisdom and grace of God in Word and Sacrament, and then enacts ministries by which the message of God's love is passed along. (Some congregations receive the message and decide to do nothing, just like the inhibitory actions of a single neuron.)

So then, it seems that many of the elements of the large system of the church—or your congregation—have their analogues in the brain itself, including its smallest parts.

A Little about the Brain Itself

Your brain can be described as about three and one half pounds of nerve cells, which is about the size of a head of cauliflower. It looks and feels like a big glob of nicely firmed tofu. It's attached to your skull by small ligaments and cushioned by a thin layer of fluid. The nerve cells are gathered together in identifiable structures—some scientists estimate as many as 800—that govern every function of the human body. These structures are comprised of about 50 different kinds of neurons that number about 100,000,000,000—that's one hundred billion. (Their synaptic interconnections exceed the estimated number of stars in our universe!) The extensions on your brain cells can be as long as one meter, although most are less than a millimeter in length. The width of a neuron measures less than one-tenth of a millimeter. (We're talking about hair-widths here!)

One end of a neuron is called the axon; on the other end are tentacle-like dendrites (DEN-drytes), as many as 100,000 per neuron. The dendrites receive chemical information from other neurons. The cell body processes the information and transmits it to other neurons via an electrical charge that travels along the axon. The axon passes the information across a tiny gap to the receptive dendrite(s) of other neurons. We call that place (or moment) a synapse (SIN-apps), or sometimes "the firing" of the synapse. On average, a brain neuron forms about 1,000 synaptic connections.

In addition to neurons, your brain contains about one trillion glial (GLEE-uhl) cells of several kinds. Glial cells don't fire in synapses, but serve other functions including those that seem to enable the work of the neurons. (See chapters 2 and 3 for further description of these cells and their work.)

Your brain can be divided into several important regions or systems:

- The subcortical regions —encompassing principally the finger-size brainstem immediately above the spinal cord, and the cerebellum (sehr-uh-BELL-uhm) immediately behind it—the bump at the back of your brain.
- The cerebral cortex—the large, deeply folded outside layers of the brain tissue that comprise about 75 percent of your brain's mass. The cortex is divided, back to front, into the sensory and frontal lobes, and right and left into the cerebral hemispheres.
- The corpus callosum (COR-puhs coh-LOSS-uhm)—a bundle of nerves that joins the two hemispheres of the cortex at the top of your brain and
- The lower brain—a collection of small but important brain structures enfolded by the cortex's layers.

How Your Brain Works

The basic activity of your brain occurs at "synapses"—tiny gaps between neurons, about one millionth of a centimeter wide. A simple way to describe a synapse is the place where—and moment when—an electrical or chemical signal leaps from cell to cell.

When the pulse of energy arrives at the synapse, calcium ions trigger the release of neurotransmitters, which are molecules that actually cross the gap from the axons of one cell to the dendrites of the next nerve cell, where they dock before activating that cell to pass along the energy. At the present time, over 60 kinds of neurotransmitter molecules have been identified, from amino acid derivatives to gases. Some of the more familiar neurotransmitters are nitric oxide, dopamine (DOPE-uh-meen), serotonin (sehr-uh-TONE-ihn), and oxytocin (ox-ee-TOSS-ihn).

These molecules exist in other places in your body, but in your brain they enable various strengths—or degrees of efficiency—of synapses. The stronger the synapse, the more likely the packet of energy will be passed along. The repeated firing of specific neuronal combinations results in habituation and memory. ("Neurons that fire together wire together" is the simplest way to remember this phenomenon.) As a kind of balancing force, some neurons function as inhibitory cells, slowing down or stopping the pulses of energy.

Brain Fact

The axons and dendrites in the brain form an interconnected tangle of constantly changing connections. There are more possible interconnections among these cells than there are atoms in the known universe.

The speed of synapse firing is relatively slow—thousandths of a second—compared to the speed at which other chemical reactions occur. The pulse of synaptic energy moves through the neuronal maze at about 200 miles an hour.

Each of your brain's neurons may have from 1 to 10,000 possible connections with other neurons, which means that the theoretical number of possible connections among all the neurons approaches 40 quadrillion. Given the sheer number of possible connections at different levels of synapse strength, it is difficult to think or speak about your brain without the matter getting complex or even unfathomable. The phrase "fearfully and wonderfully made" comes to mind.

Your Brain's Organization

Your brain's structures are organized into larger systems, organized to accomplish two major tasks: to regulate the body's systems and to recognize and respond to external stimuli. The systems include the following:

- Your subcortical areas—the brainstem, cerebellum and related systems—unconsciously monitor and regulate bodily activities such as digestion, respiration, and circulation. Sometimes the phrase "autonomic system" is used to describe these coordinated functions.
- Your forebrain—also called the neocortex or cerebral cortex—is comprised of six thin layers of brain cells covering the outside of your brain. Your forebrain comprises about 75 percent of your total brain and deals with the external environment.

A comparison to your congregation's organization may be helpful. What percentage of your congregation's efforts—budget, program, energy, mission—is allocated to internal maintenance, and what per-

Big Question

How might discoveries in neuroscience contribute answers to the difficult questions surrounding the termination of pregnancy by abortion?

centage is assigned to external matters? Another way of asking the question is, "How much attention do you pay to the internal well-being of your congregation, and how much attention is devoted to your congregation's external ministries?" (You'll see these questions paraphrased in several other places in this book, so you might want to start thinking about them right away.)

Two other brain structures will be important to our considerations in this book:

- Your brain's pleasure centers—the hypothalamus (high-poh-THAL-uh-muss) and the nucleus accumbens (NEW-clee-uhs ACK-uhm-behns). These structures are sometimes called the "reward and pleasure centers."
- The hippocampus (hip-poh-CAM-puhs), which seems to be your brain's memory center.

For future reference, it is becoming increasingly obvious that most functions of the brain are not limited to a single brain structure. As scientists unravel the mysteries of the brain's functions, they find more and more how various human activities—such as praying, planning or reading—occur all over the brain in a unified, coordinated way. For example, you "smell" in your brain's olfactory bulb, the amygdala (uh-MIGG-duh-luh), the hypothalamus, hippocampus, and the cortex. You know and feel emotions all over your brain, not just in the sensory lobes. The important matter of paying attention may require the fine-tuned cooperation of almost every structure of your brain.

Developing Brains

Your brain began developing within eight weeks after conception. Primitive nerve cells called "neuroblasts" grew at the rate of 250,000 every minute during the first weeks and months. Your brain's rapid development continued *in utero* and during the first year of your life. Although the rate slowed after this time, your brain cells grew and connected until you were the age of 20.

The growth happened in two general stages, one between birth and age 10, and the other between ages 11 and 20. In the first stage—characterized by a gradually developing competence—your brain developed motor skills, language, good manners, and rapid reflexive responses. You were learning to be a human being. This growth took place primarily at the back of the brain, and helped you to recognize the nature of immediate challenges.

During the second stage, your frontal lobes organized and connected so that you could respond to challenges. As an older child and adolescent, you learned how to become a productive, reproductive human being; you developed sexuality and commitment, vocation, reflective and moral thought, and the capacity for delayed gratification.

During all stages of life, your brain is "plastic"—capable of rapid learning and change—and is influenced by both environment and heredity. You exercise your free will, making decisions about how you will adapt to your environment, thus influencing the specific ways your brain can continue its development.

What's Brain Science?

Under a variety of names—neurobiology, neuroscience, neuropsychiatry, neurochemistry—brain research has created a bona fide physical science over many decades. Observation and experimentation have increased in sophistication and accuracy since the early history of brain research.

❗ Trying It Out

Fire up that Web browser of yours, type in any of the terms or ideas you find in this book, and see what pops up. For starters, try *amygdala*. Two sites that continue to be helpful are Brain Connection (http://www.brainconnection. com. Click on "Explore.") and BrainInfo Database (http://www.braininfo. rprc.washington.edu).

In those days, scientists determined the function of brain structures by studying brains damaged by stroke, tumor, or trauma. They would try to correlate the loss of a specific function with damage to a particular area of the brain. Some of the experimentation included techniques such as split-brain research (where the corpus callosum was surgically severed) or removal of parts of the brain.

Today, scientists have added to their toolboxes a range of brain-imaging technologies that reveal what happens as the brain is engaged in a particular task, such as meditating, reading a book on brain science, or dreaming. These procedures are usually called scans, and include positron-emission tomography (PET), functional magnetic resonance imagery (fMRI) and single photon emission computed tomography (SPECT).

Another facet of research focuses on single nerve cells that are grown in lab conditions. These efforts have yielded many of the most fascinating, close-up discoveries. For example, we now know that embryonic brain cells actually migrate to the places in the brain where they will live. We can also describe the chemical composition of synapses down to the level of atoms.

The amount of information scientists have about the brain increases exponentially every year, and the maze of theories connected to that data grows more complicated as well.

A major difficulty remains, however. We cannot describe with the reasonable certainty required of "science" what is occurring in the big picture. For example, we know that nerve cells can regenerate themselves and which chemicals are involved. But we don't know what ultimately triggers that process and under what circumstances; and we don't really know what "cell regeneration" might mean for its wider applications in daily human existence.

Also problematic is that the actions of a single cell—or the chemicals of which it is composed—can be more easily examined than interconnected bundles of neurons. But the actions and reactions of that one cell hardly describe the way it might behave in a brain that is working in concert with its chaotic context. It is as inaccurate and unhelpful to reduce our understanding of the human brain down to the actions of a single cell as it is to describe a congregation by the actions or character of one of its members.

Because we cannot ethically undertake experiments on living human brains, we may never be able to fathom completely the workings of the brain with any exactitude or certainty. This is why metaphors and visual images of the

Brain Fact

Another way single neurons are examined: if a mini-electrode is inserted next to a specific neuron— in patients already undergoing open-brain surgery—it is possible for fMRI (functional magnetic resonance imaging) scanners to record that neuron's activity by measuring increases in blood flow.

brain and its functions continue to be useful tools in understanding the bigger pictures of brain function and interconnectivity. For example, "synapse firing"—which suggests a sudden sparking of chemicals—is easier to understand than descriptions of "glutamate binding to post-synaptic nuerons with differing levels of excitatory or inhibitory potentiation."

Because your brain is highly adaptive, integrated, individualized, and infinitely complex, it can best be described with theories and metaphors that seem to take into account an array of facts. For example, some scientists have tried to integrate the complex nature of brain science into the broad theories of quantum physics. They see in the human brain the patterns and interactions that could be explained by complexity physics. In their view, the actions of the brain may be explained as self-ordering mechanisms, and brain science may illustrate exquisitely the inadequacies of Cartesian cause-and-effect explanations.

A Useful Science

Facts about the human brain are multiplying rapidly and starting to make sense together. Like iron filings sticking to a magnet, pieces of brain science seem to be attracted to theoretical propositions or theorems. As the theorems themselves sort into loose collections of interrelated truth—for example, the theorem family "use it or lose it"—brain science can be increasingly useful in many areas of life. So educators work with brain-based learning strategies, nutritionists examine the effects of diet on brain development, psychiatrists prescribe drugs that restore depleted brain chemicals, marital counselors learn the neurobiology of love, social scientists reexamine change theory as a function of brain plasticity, and manufacturers look at how your brain experiences pleasure when your stomach contains specific brands of soft drinks.

Judging from the constant appearance of brain-related matters in the popular media, it's evident that leaders of business, government, and other human enterprises are working hard to integrate brain science into contemporary life, or how it might be lived in the future. Sooner or later the church will become part of that enterprise.

The Simple Proposition Revisited

The simple proposition mentioned earlier in this book's preface can be both intriguing and difficult to prove. Brain science can be helpful in understanding the workings of congregations. In this book we'll explore

Knowledge is never values-neutral, and brain science falls into that general category. Our task as God's people is not to avoid and condemn the facts or theories of brain science, but to search for God's creating and sustaining hand in these matters and our responsibility to serve God with this knowledge. Our work is not to build intellectual fortresses around our theology or our Bible so that we can debunk brain science in a flurry of proof-texting or a barrage of theological stone-throwing. Instead, we can engage this particular field of knowledge with gratitude to the God by whose original and continuing power the human brain works. We can appropriate what we can understand into the purposes to which God calls us, particularly in our congregations.

Brain Fact

Dangerous knowledge may be a kind of urban myth, presumed to exist but hard to actually find anywhere. See what happens when you ask the questions, "What might make knowledge dangerous?" or "What contemporary field of knowledge do you think is dangerous?" or "What used to be considered dangerous knowledge but is no longer labeled that way?" My prediction? The answers you get will be all over the map.

Where This Book Will Lead You

Just in case this is the first book you've read about brain science, pure or applied, take these assurances and challenges with you into the chapters that follow:

- None of us quite yet knows where all of this will lead. By reading this book you join an exploration that's just getting started.
- Nothing in this book can be demonstrated to be important or useful unless you try out the questions and possible actions embedded in these pages.
- As you uncover new facts or discern the meaning of new theories here, you'll find new wisdom about what you do in your congregation. Maybe you'll find new curiosity.
- What you read here may surprise you, perhaps even delight your

that proposition together, presuming that the theories of brain science
and the facts that fit into those theories, however untidy they are—c
also be useful for understanding the life of the church. As you put in
practice what you read here, you'll become a verifying agent for this n
branch of applied brain science.

A Few Words about Dangerous Knowledge

As you read this book, you may wonder whether playing with brai
science leads to playing God. You could start to see brain science as
kind of dangerous knowledge—nearly incomprehensible facts whos
barely understood applications could quickly get out of control. Yo
might think, "Once we know about how brains work, won't we b
tempted to manipulate others, for personal gain or with evil intent?" Yo
might remember how bigots and other miscreants have co-opted othe
branches of scientific knowledge for their misguided crusades.

The answer? You may be right, just as you could be right about
research into disease prevention, astronomy, geology, or genetics. All
knowledge can be dangerous unless we presume the loving, guiding
hand of a grace-filled God from whom the knowledge first emanated,
and the Holy Spirit's work to preserve God's people in faithful service to
God's purposes. Given only human ingenuity and egocentricity, any
knowledge, skill, and experience could be directed toward the building
of contemporary Towers of Babel, ziggurats that testify only to the glo-
ries of human enterprise and kick God to the side of the road.

The problem is not with the knowledge itself but the self-gratifying,
ego-laden purposes it might serve. So medical research could be seen
primarily as a miracle of healing or a way to line the pockets of investors
in pharmaceutical firms. Stem-cell research could be considered a
promising avenue for the curing of a variety of debilitating diseases or an
immoral invasion of the lives of the unborn. Electronic technology
could be viewed as an inspiration for new forms of human communication or a way to debase the creative spirit. Brain imaging could unlock
cures for brain-based diseases or be used to filter out mental undesir-
ables from insurance coverage or employment.

spirit with new possibilities. It might give you a little more energy for your congregational leadership.

- It's good to approach brain science with prayerful humility. You serve the God who fashioned your brain into something wonderful.
- Take notes about what you read; mark up the book with your questions and comments. Make your own revised edition.
- Supplement this book with new facts, newer theories, and questions that have just emerged.
- Don't worry if you feel confused. That's how we all got started.
- Read around in this book—it loops around itself in several ways—like you would a collection of readings. Start with what interests you and move forward and backward through the pages like you would on a Web site. When something clicks, stay there awhile. If it doesn't, come back later.

Looking Ahead

In the next chapter, I'll take you through some of the interesting places where brain science meets theology. We'll look at matters such as sin, the nature of religious experience, forgiveness, idolatry, and prayer. We'll revisit some Scripture passages that connect well with brain science. We'll even name some of the problems. Get ready for your reading by thinking about the following question: "What's the difference between faith and knowledge?" Have fun with your answers.

Exploring Further

With a small group of people, examine any of the following questions or try some of the suggested activities. They may help you make better sense out of what you've read in this chapter.

1. Find "astounding" facts or ideas about brain science in current news magazines, newspapers, or journals. For a sure-fire place to start, look at popular science magazines such as *Discover* or *Scientific American*. Talk with someone about what you find amazing.

2. What would happen in your congregation if you suggested that congregational leaders study brain science as a way of understanding
   how to be leaders? How do you know?
3. What parts of this introduction are already out of date or undergoing careful scrutiny?
4. Who do you know personally who could talk intelligently about
   these matters and who you could trust with your deepest questions?
5. Why did you first decide to read this book? What do you hope to
   gain from your reading?

Chapter 1

The Lord Gave
Each of Us a Mind

Belief and Knowledge

ON THE FACE OF IT, the proposition is obvious: our minds come from God's creative hand. The writer of Psalm 33 knew that, and so penned the words that, millennia later, have become this chapter's title, "The Lord Gave Each of Us a Mind." What comes to your mind after you accept the psalmist's faithful statement, though, is not so obvious. The relationship between God and the human brain is not easily understood or simply expressed.

When it comes to theology and brain science, questions such as "How?" "Why?" "Who?" and "When?" aren't easily answered with generic statements about God's originating power. "What does this mean?" requires responses that intertwine like the root tendrils of orchard trees. It's not easy to explain how both theology and brain science shed light on each other's realities, enriching each other's truth. But that's what I'm going to do in this chapter, as hard as it might seem to be.

In the following pages I invite you to wrap your God-given mind around some of the fascinating connections between brain science and theology. When this chapter is complete, perhaps the connections will be stronger for you. Perhaps you'll find more "obvious propositions" that

17

could become chapter titles in the book *you* write about applied brain science.

Big Picture: Belief and Knowledge

"Wow!" is a good place to start with both belief and knowledge, the big ideas for this chapter. The "Wow!" that comes with belief is the amazing proposition that you're capable of trusting what and who exists beyond the limits of your knowledge. The "Wow!" that comes with knowledge is an equally astounding fact. Billions of pieces of infinitely small data are assembled by other brains into manageable chunks of truth that your brain, in turn, integrates into its own mental maps. Belief and knowledge share another "Wow!" Truth nests in both places.

There's more to belief and knowledge than "Wow!" and so I invite you to consider how these paired elements of life play themselves out, first in your brain and then in your congregation.

Although brain science and theology share similar qualities—discussed later in this chapter—there are fundamental differences between the underlying matters of belief and knowledge.

When you believe, you accept something as true—sufficient enough to cause you to take action—even though there may not be sufficiently conclusive evidence to validate that assertion. Belief is always a tautology, a circular logic reinforced by its own propositions and emotions. So there is no empirical evidence for life after death, or the superiority of Christian ethics as compared to the ethics of Islam. There are only shreds of brain science that "prove" the value of one supposedly "brain-based" reading methodology over another. No "sure-fire magic bullets" for renewing congregations are based on verifiable, valid, reliable, and replicable evidence about their short- or long-term effects.

Knowledge, on the other hand, seems to rest on a body of evidence that is accepted as measurable fact. Knowledge is also true and also invites your action or reaction. Knowledge is also exclusive, not necessarily because of circular logic, but because most factual data tends to exclude other data. A neuron cannot be alive and dead at the same moment; Islam and Christianity cannot be both older and younger than each other; students cannot score both poorly and excellently on the same reading test; a congregation cannot be both gaining and losing its financial support at the same moment.

Big Question

In your life, what's the difference between "I believe" and "I know"? When do they blend? Where's God in "I believe" and in "I know"?

When belief and knowledge take on spiritual tones, the differences can be accentuated by the passions attached to each. Believers in Christ as Savior care deeply about sharing their version of good news to the exclusion of other views of salvation; creationists are deeply passionate about their view of literal Scripture and the shortcomings of science; brain scientists are deeply insistent that the bits and pieces of their work not turn into ill-formed propositions or patterns of religio-political thought.

Your brain acts on the truth it finds in both belief and knowledge. Knowledge-based reactivity is easy to spot: your brain checks every stimulus against preexisting mental maps stored in long-term memory. "Verifiable fact" for your brain may be as simple as that. "Belief" is more difficult to name as a function of the brain. (I'll introduce you to "neurotheology" a little later in the chapter, which may help.) Perhaps it's enough for you and I to believe that belief exists in the brain.

Sometimes leaders comingle belief and knowledge. This intermixing may be inevitable, necessary and good, if only because neither belief nor knowledge can carry the weight of truth by itself—at least not in a modern or post-modern world. My own parochial school upbringing relied on the propositional constructs of Luther's Small Catechism, replete with the comforting presence of scores of biblical references supporting each proposed truth. My teachers and parents wanted me to be filled with faith and belief, but they used belief-based Scriptures as proof for the knowledge foundation they hoped would house my beliefs. In their view, "knowing God and knowing truth" seemed to require both belief and knowledge and so they exposed me to both.

Belief and knowledge show up in your congregation as surely as they show up in your brain. It wouldn't take you long to assess how belief and knowledge are the primary cause(s) for actions your congregation takes. For example, your congregation's strong belief in the primacy of evangelism may be so strong that you organize large-scale congregational programming toward that end—despite the verifiable fact that only about 10 percent of Christians self-identify personal witnessing as a primary spiritual gift. In that case, you would take action based on your belief, not your knowledge. Using the same example, you could decide *not* to engage in any kind of evangelism effort—except with an identified 10 percent of your congregation's members—because of the statistic I cited. In that case, knowledge would compel your lack of action, a kind of action in itself.

Let me mix belief and knowledge in two other axioms about congregations. I believe both observations to be true from my years of informal data-collecting:

1. The more that congregations—and their leaders—insist on accumulating overwhelming empirical evidence—a kind of knowledge—before they take action, the less action they take.
2. Congregations that act primarily on their passionate beliefs may be immediately successful but eventually burn out because members haven't assessed all the facts before deciding to act.

Yes, the observations are contradictory. But they illustrate how difficult it can be for you to choose the bases upon which you make decisions about your congregation's mission and ministry, and about what it means to be a leader.

Trying It Out

Talk to some present and former leaders in your congregation, and ask them if (or how) my two observations here have shown themselves in your congregation's life.

As you move into this chapter, carry both belief and knowledge with you as tools by which you'll carry out your calling to be a congregational leader. Switch gears with me now as we start moving toward the relationship between theology and brain science.

Stepping Around Reductionism

Before looking at theology and brain science, I have to talk about reductionism, an irksome problem that bothers most varieties of science, much like fleas bother most varieties of dogs. In brain science, reductionism—sometimes called materialism—is any effort to explain or extrapolate the workings of the entire brain from the workings of a single cell or single brain structure. In neuroscience, reductionism shows up in two major issues:

1. Whether "the mind" can be reduced to "the brain."
2. Whether consciousness is more than the sum of the brain's individual functions.

It would be easy to reduce brain science or theological thought to arrangements of chemical compounds with confusing names, or the sequenced firing of neurons along synaptic pathways. One example of too-easy reductionism: "Sin? It's nothing more than the so-called reptillian and mammalian brains trying to protect the body they live in."

If taken to its logical extreme, materialistic thought reduces the truth of theology and the value of religious enterprise to measurable results. A familiar example: "Numerical growth in a congregation's membership rolls is proof of its health." Another, perhaps outrageous example: "The value of brain science to theology can be measured by the number of people who buy that wonderful book, *Your Brain Goes to Church*."

Even friendly reductionism—the idea that religion and faith are nothing more than natural human activities—might easily lead you down the wrong path. You could easily believe that the brain sciences (especially the cognitive sciences) are the knowledge base that explains mysteries of the faith such as Jesus' dual nature, the resurrection of the body, or your feeling of God's presence in worship. (You might also hope that brain science would fully account for the small and niggling issues of church life, such as why ushers sometimes forget which pew was handed which offering plate, why some worshipers sit in the same spot each Sunday, or why babies cry only during the quiet times in sermons!)

There are times when a materialistic or reductionistic approach is helpful, however. Sometimes you can find exquisite evidence of God's abundant work in seemingly small details of theology or brain science. For example, it's fascinating to look at the biochemistry of *fear* and *love* in the light of 1 John 4:18 ("Perfect love casts out fear") and to find out that John's statement is both a theological principle and an accurate description of the neurobiology of fear dispersal.

Another benefit of materialistic explanations is that they can link a variety of previously disconnected phenomena. My current favorite? How the biology of attention—and inattention—explains such subjects as daydreaming during sermons. (See chapter 3 for further details.)

In this chapter, I'll try to avoid using completely reductionist approaches to demonstrate theology's relationship with neurobiology. Such "proofs" don't seem to carry enough intellectual freight—"too quickly simplified" comes to mind. I am willing, however, to take an alternative approach. I prefer to trust that truth can exist even where it cannot be proven because I trust the mercy and power of a God beyond proving. There will be times when that's as far as my mind is able to go.

Brain Fact

Neurons are *not* little off-on switches. In a way, each neuron operates like a brain inside a brain, taking in information from other neurons, sifting and prioritizing the information, even ignoring some information. The neuron then decides how, when, and where to direct that information.

Complementary Endeavors

Neurotheology is an emerging body of inquiry that cross-pollinates theology and neuroscience. These two areas of human endeavor may be coming together as an interrelated discipline of study. Both share certain characteristics:

- Neurobiology and theology attempt to make sense of important elements of life; for example, what it means to be truly human.
- Both brain science and theology are hard to express in purely empirical terms. (How can self-awareness or sin be fully measured?)

- Both depend on *a priori* assumptions for their fundamental values—"I think, therefore I am" or "God pre-exists."
- Brain science and theology attract devoted adherents who construct scientific and religious organizations from truths they hold to be true.

Trying It Out

Look at the Yellow Pages or a Sunday newspaper and identify advertisements from churches that incorporate *science* into their names. Ask around, and see how much your friends and colleagues know about these churches and their beliefs.

You can look at the "friendly hug" of neurobiology and theology from the viewpoint of the other. Theology benefits from brain science, for example, when religious experiences such as prayer, meditation, or forgiveness are measured by technologies such as fMRI (functional magnetic resonance imaging) and PET (positron emission tomography). Brain science benefits from theology because theology can offer neuroscience the constructs it needs to explain seemingly imponderable or unrelated brain functions. For example, *soul* might become the guiding metaphor that most adequately describes human consciousness.

Big Question

What characterizes the beliefs or behaviors of Christians for whom "the relationship of science and theology" is not so friendly, or those who see both fields of human endeavor as diametrically opposed? How do you know?

Most people today accept a kind of scientific theology. In this way of thinking, scientific inquiry is not seen as the enemy of theology, nor is theology used to limit legitimate scientific inquiry. Instead, the questions and answers of each discipline inform the questions and answers of the other. Belief and knowledge can coexist. For example, both brain science and theology benefit from each other's descriptions of altruism (selfless kindness).

In this next section, I'm going to explore some places where brain science and theology meet at the same crossroads. The subjects I'll examine include the following:

- Prayer
- Religious experience
- The nature of God
- Original and ongoing sinfulness
- Freedom of will and salvation
- Forgiveness as a state of mind

After I'm finished with these ideas, I'll invite you to have fun speculating about some edgy propositions, and I'll look at some Bible passages and stories from the viewpoint of brain science.

Prayer in Science and Theology

The friendly interplay between theology and brain science is probably best seen in prayer (which includes deep meditation). The physical and spiritual benefits of prayer have been fairly well established—stress levels are reduced, immune systems are strengthened, lives are healed or otherwise changed, God's presence is experienced. During prayer, blood pressure, heart rate, and cortisol levels are lowered. The deepest yearnings of the human spirit are given voice, and courage and comfort are received. For neuroscientists, theologians, and those who pray, prayer is a measurable, beneficial act.

But what, really, is prayer? That was the biological and theological question on the minds of neurobiologists Andrew Newberg and Eugene D'Aquili as they attempted to find neural explanations for religious experience. In their attempts to understand both the biology and theology of prayer—they coined the term *neurotheology*—they applied the technologies of brain imaging to the question, "What happens inside brains when people pray?" Their findings were similar across a broad spectrum of prayer-like spiritual practices. Deep prayer or meditation quiets the parietal (pah-RYE-ih-tuhl) lobe of the cerebral cortex. The body's quieting and attention-arousing systems are both activated and held in delicate balance.

In their book detailing this work—*Why God Won't Go Away: Brain Science and the Biology of Belief*—Newberg and D'Aquili conjectured that prayer induces this balanced state of mind. They called it "absolute unitary being" (AUB), a quiescent, transcendent sense of unity with God easily seen on the screens of brain imaging machines. By respecting both theology and brain science, Newberg and D'Aquili thus signaled how to approach the relationship between these two branches of God-given knowledge.

At this point I want to raise some yellow flags, both scientific and theological. First (and always?) we must beware of the temptation to reduce prayer to only electrical or chemical impulses observed in specific areas of the brain. Scientifically, this inquiry into prayer invites other, more complex investigation. For example, we don't yet understand what happens in brains before and after prayer, its causes and effects. It may be impossible to measure kinds or amounts of prayer.

At the same time, some familiar theological dilemmas might be stirred up. Ancient heresies can get dressed up in neurobiological clothing but the propositions will still be questionable or idolatrous. For example, *absolute unitary being* may be only a short metaphysical distance from *universalism,* the doctrine that all humans are saved because religious thought is basically similar across the spectrum of beliefs. Another short conceptual walk turns prayer into a technique like just any other self-improvement fad-of-the-month.

These necessary cautions notwithstanding, it seems to be a good and godly enterprise to continue studying prayer. Reliance on God's power in prayer will not be destroyed by images from a single photon emission computed tomography (SPECT) camera. Instead, those colorful images may turn out to be places where we can see God's work in human enterprise.

Trying It Out

Survey religious communications you encounter—television programs, newsletters from your congregation, denominational publications, advertisements—to see if prayer has turned into just another one of the countless methods by which personal development is guaranteed. Look for step-by-step approaches, methods and systems that promise results, and ratings scales of proposed effectiveness.

Religious Experience Redux

One of the most pressing debates within the church swirls around religious experience. There is a wide gulf between those for whom religious experience—usually accompanied by high emotion—is essential to their theology, and those for whom religious experience is suspect. Mystics, fundamentalists, traditionalists, practitioners of New Age spirituality, mainline political activists—each group seeks to prove or justify its positions and practices regarding religious experience. No branch of the Christian family seems to be swayed by the philosophical or theological arguments of other groups. Many people outside faith communities suspect that religious experience is a pathology of the human condition, claimed and practiced by essentially dysfunctional people as a substitute for logic and reason.

Brain science might eventually help settle the question, as researchers study states of the spiritual mind and identify recognizable and replicable patterns on brain-wave tests. For example, "the generous giver" or "actively praising worshiper" might become familiar patterns on a PET scan or electroencephalogram (EEG) monitor. "Whole brain involvement" may emerge as a standard or desired state of mind, so that varieties of religious experience could be compared with each other.

Larger questions—"Is religious experience a natural state?" "Can the brain be stimulated or manipulated to engage in religious experiences?" and "What do these experiences mean?"—cannot be easily answered by science alone. And so science knocks at the doors of theology, seeking wisdom (or perhaps better questions).

The Nature of God

Try as you might, it's just not feasible—or defensible—to use neuroscience to describe the nature of God. Still, as you become more familiar with brain science, you might want to know if there are neurobiological answers to questions such as the following:

- If I'm "fearfully and wonderfully made," how does my brain perceive a fearful and wonderful God?
- With your brain in mind, what does it mean to be "made in God's image" (Gen. 1:27)?
- What newer brain science metaphors might open "the mind (or depths) of God" (1 Corinthians 2:10-11)?
- How or when does "God's mind" change (compare 1 Sam. 15:29 and Joel 2:14)?
- What brain activity is involved in the idolatry of thinking you're just enough like God to be in charge of your life?
- How could humans have "the mind of Christ" (Phil. 2:5)?

These may be difficult questions to pose, if only because they skate up to the place where we run out of words. You can hope that the blending of neurobiology and theology into a coordinated discipline of thought—after all, that's what neurotheology is all about—will result in better answers. Perhaps you'll learn just to be satisfied with better questions.

When you examine your brain with theology in mind, you can expect to scrutinize ideas such as, "Is there a 'God-spot' in the human brain, a single, hard-wired center for God-directed thought or other religious experience?" Another hard question: "Is 'God' just a way of describing 'the mind of the world,' the collective intelligence and psychic energy of the entire world?" (Writers of science fiction have had fun with that idea for years!)

It's good that you proceed with caution. As neurotheology develops its methods and refines its findings, you may again find yourself flirting with ancient heresies such as pantheism and gnosticism. Brain science may enter the difficult debates about panentheism and process theology; that is, God has a constant relation with the world and may also be dependent on its reality. Another place for neurotheology to explore is "intelligent design," a strain of theological inquiry currently bound up in questions about the origin of the universe. As time goes on, you'll ask harder questions whose answers will themselves generate as-yet-unknown fields of inquiry. An understanding of God as "totally Other" may yet turn out to be the most accurate (and most humbling) way to approach the whole subject.

Original and Ongoing Sinfulness

For centuries, philosophers and theologians have tussled with each other over "human nature." On one side have been those who argue that humans are sinful from birth. (Augustine, Calvin, Luther and Freud come to mind.) On the other side is an array of thinkers who have taken a more positive or neutral view of basic human nature. (Marx and theologians in the Orthodox tradition might be included in that group.)

Brain Fact

A primary source of neurobiologists' understanding of social and sexual behavior comes from their work with one strain of prairie vole, a mouse-like rodent. What makes the vole especially valuable? Like most humans who bond in marriage, this strain of voles mates for life.

With the advent of sociobiology in the 1970s, scientific inquiry about human nature took a different tack. One branch of sociobiology called *memetics* proposed the existence of *memes,* which are discreet bits of shared cultural information hardwired into our brains over eons. (Examples of memes might be vengeance, self-preservation, or kinship.) According to memetic theory, these "infectious cultural replicators" (or "thought genes") carry over from one generation to the next, primarily through imitation of others. For sociobiologists, human nature, however good or evil it might be, might be nothing more or less than the accumulation of those traits over time.

Modern brain theory and brain science entered the discussion about 30 years ago as well. Neurophysiologist Paul MacLean proposed the existence of a *triune brain,* the notion that the brain is composed of three interrelated-yet-competing structures (the reptillian and mammalian brains, and the cortex). Some theologians proposed that MacClean's theory explained original sin—the notion that humans are born predisposed to a baseline selfishness that can exclude God and all others. The

Triune brain theory may also shed light on the Reformation principle of *simul justus et peccator*—that humans are simultaneously both saint and sinner.

Recent mappings of brain physiology have called into question Mac-Clean's clean lines of demarcation regarding brain structures. Still, his proposition—that the automatically defensive or protective reptillian and mammalian brains are held in check by the rational cortex—might demonstrate how redeemed sinners could continue to be susceptible to the brutish selfishness from which God's love has rescued them.

From the viewpoint of a tripartide brain, one way to categorize sin—both original and continuing—could be the excluding selfishness of the reptellian and mammalian brains, an attitude that pushes aside God and others. Because human brains are wired so that social interaction is essential to well-being, a consequence of sin—one we interpret as punishment—is the separation from others, including God, produced by self-centeredness. (As my mother used to tell my brothers and me, "Selfishness gets rewarded by selfishness.")

> **Brain Fact**
>
> *Affiliative neurocircuitry* is another way of describing the existence of the social brain, structures and functions in the human brain that help humans manage threat. Implicated in this circuitry are the hormones oxytocin, vasopressin, endorphines, and growth hormone.

What mediates sin? Altruism—selfless love of others that draws us toward them for the sake of *their* well-being—may be hardwired into the brain as surely as self-centeredness. For Christians, this sacrificial love for humanity is exemplified in the life and person of Jesus Christ. You carry his name and his message to others, as an infectious agent of God's love throughout time.

Another branch of brain science might offer an intriguing possibility for understanding sin. Continuing research into the biological mechanisms of addictions might show that our brain's pleasure center and its related structures are strong motivators for action. The pleasure center both reinforces and enables addictive behaviors. Sensitized to the addictive substance, behavior, or relationships, the brain shuts out other activities so that it can maintain its singular focus.

In light of the biology of addictions, perhaps sin as separation from God might correlate with the thought that a brain habituated on its self-satisfaction most likely cannot reach a state in which oneness with God and with others can be experienced. The sources of addictive pleasure are all around, which might explain why sin is self-perpetuating.

Also related is the theological tugging and pulling between "theologies of glory" and "the theology of the cross." Theologies of glory (prosperity, entertainment, victory, or nationalism) bring pleasure to your brain. This might explain why theologies of glory seem to be so strong and sometimes so easily accepted. It makes sense (to your brain) to continue seeking the sources of that pleasure.

Another take on the subject: your brain might naturally avoid places and sources of pain, thus making the promises of theologies of glory more apt to be widely popular. The power of fear in your brain might also work against the theology of the cross, which deals with pain and suffering. The theology of the cross may appeal, however, to the self-sacrificing or altruistic potential of the social brain—the human desire for companionship or intimacy. For brain scientists, altruism names the potential of the human brain for attitudes and behaviors centered on trust, love, community, self-sacrifice, and forgiveness.

Freedom of Will and Salvation

The subject of free will is as unresolved in brain science as it is in theology. Brain scientists disagree about consciousness, or definitions of *mind* and *brain,* which might be the closest neurobiological equivalents to free will. After centuries of debate, theologians have not come to agreement about the relationship between free will and salvation. Once again we're back to extremely difficult questions that need both theological and brain-based answers:

- Neurobiologically, what does free will consist of? How does your brain choose and how does it operate automatically?
- When and how does your brain, by its choices, shape the contexts by which it will later be shaped?
- What might *salvation* mean neurobiologically? How does your brain

identify situations or problems beyond its capacity to solve? Can your brain choose to correct its own habituated sinfulness?

- What brain functions or mechanisms does God use to help you accept God's grace and appropriate Christ's saving actions for your redemption?

Big Question

How do *free will* and *God's indwelling* square with the notion that the human brain responds and acts automatically to protect and maintain the organism in which it lives?

Freedom of will probably depends on a basic awareness of one's self. (A simple way to think of self-awareness is as thoughts and words residing in the cortex.) In recent years, though, we have come to see that the limbic structures and the so-called lower brain participate in a kind of subliminal self-awareness (perhaps consciousness?) that coordinates your brain and other systems of the body with each other. The following questions arise immediately:

- How could your unspoken or unthought self-awareness be involved in free will?
- How do billions of neurons fire in predetermined patterns that are at the same time aware of the "will" of other parts of your brain?
- How might confession and absolution work neurobiologically, as shapers of self-awareness, consciousness, or free will?

Brain science or theology alone cannot explain to any degree of certainty what is taking place when philosophers and theologians speak of free will or salvation (or definitions of *mind* and *brain,* consciousness, or self-awareness). Each body of inquiry depends on the other.

Forgiveness as State of Mind

The word *forgiveness* calls to mind an extended family of doctrinal ideals and behaviors at the heart of human community. As a gift of the

Holy Spirit, forgiveness begins with God's grace. Forgiveness is a way God's redemptive love perseveres in human culture, perhaps in human minds.

Most Christians who believe in the power of forgiveness and who daily practice its principles understand that forgiveness is a pragmatic benefit of the Christian life. Forgiveness is real, not only as a redemptive force in human relationships but also as a sign of God's continuing presence in the world. When you receive it, forgiveness is a gift beyond description. When you offer it, forgiveness lifts away the hurt, sorrow, shame, and guilt that another person may have needlessly been carrying.

Forgiveness is an interesting biological phenomenon. Although there is no forgiveness gene, and although forgiveness seems to work against your brain's self-centered tendencies, it may be hardwired in the human brain as one kind of altruism. It is possible that moments of forgiving and being forgiven are accompanied by great emotional relief and a rush of the brain's feel-good chemicals (endorphins, serotonin, dopamine). Because these chemicals help your brain to work, forgiving actions may encourage you to continue forgiving actions. As they become habitual—nueronal "highways" are formed by repeated behaviors—forgiving actions can become a state of mind, a preferred pathway for your brain's thought, activity, and even self-identity.

Brain Fact

During the early 1980s, neuroscientists discovered that once the human brain focuses on a particular task or subject, it can, in later, similar circumstances, devote less effort to that same task or subject.

Permit me one important sidenote about the admonition for forgiving persons to forgive and forget. While it is possible for humans to renounce anger and revenge indefinitely and to empathize with others who are in need of forgiveness, forgetting hurt and pain may not be biologically possible. In one sense, your brain does not forget anything, and mental maps of anticipated reactions, such as punishment or revenge, are not easily wiped clean.

What may happen instead of forgetting is something called *secondary attenuation*. In this neuronal state, a secondary stimulus covers over (distracts from?) the brain's reaction to a previous stimulus. So perfect love casts out fear, a soft word turns away wrath, and forgiveness overlays hurt. Something better covers something sorrowful, just like love covers a multitude of sins. (Yes, these biblical allusions illustrate how some theological statements also work well as statements about your brain.)

Quick Conjectures

Just for fun, let me show you some snapshots—photographed with the lens of brain science—of some common elements of Christian theology and see how the pictures turn out. When developed, some of the pictures may necessarily take on reductionist hues, if only for a few moments.

The Soul

Consciousness, self-identity, and attention are part of a constellation of brain-related topics that take their place alongside a possible theological equivalent—the soul.

Brain scientists have rarely ventured beyond questions about consciousness and its cousins, except for one brilliant scientist and philospher. Francis Crick, codiscoverer of the DNA sequence and its implications, wrote a splendidly convoluted work several years ago in which he invited readers into his astonishing hypothesis, that *soul* could be equated with *self-perception,* and that that activity coincided with the brain's ability to see. Crick's seeming reductionism notwithstanding, brain science cannot presently explain the neurobiology of soul-related themes.

Faith

Are you hardwired to believe in God? The evidence is sketchy and hardly conclusive. Still, mystical experiences have always been part of the human condition, and for millennia, people have developed theistic explanations for every facet of life. One way to think about *faith* in neurobiological terms might be the idea of *neuronal potentiation*. This term identifies a state of readiness, expectancy, and capacity for action in nueronal bundles that exists well in advance of any stimulus. Perhaps that readiness could be rephrased as "the assurance of things hoped for, the conviction of things not seen" (Heb. 11:1).

Law and Gospel

Pronouncements of the Law arouse fear, if only about deserved punishment. At the same time, the Law's condemnations may be the perfect biological preparation for the good news of God's action in your life, including the best news of all: you're saved from the power of sin and death. When they work in tandem, Law and Gospel may release a believing brain from what Luther described as "terrors of conscience" (and attendant brain mechanisms such as fleeing, fighting, or freezing). After fear subsides—because of the presence of good news—the brain is flooded with feel-good neurotransmitters. Without each other, both Law and Gospel probably fall flat emotionally, incapable alone of converting the brain from its purely selfish preoccupation.

Generosity

It now seems evident that most human brains are hardwired for cooperative behavior, altruism, trust, hope, or love. Generosity might be a way by which these attitudes are expressed toward others, both for their good and for the good of the giver. Because human existence is dependent on the social brain—those parts of the brain that engender beneficial contact with other humans—generosity may be a primary means by which beneficial social networks are established and maintained. Philanthropists and stewardship leaders speak of the giver's need to give, and in that statement may describe a biological propensity for generosity. From a theological standpoint, generosity is connected with deep gratitude—to God and to others—which is, in turn, connected with prayer, harmonious living with others, and unity with others. Perhaps AUB—see the earlier section on prayer—can also be experienced in acts of generosity.

Temptation

One mantra of brain science goes like this, "What you can imagine, you can do; what you can do, you can imagine." For example, the mere consideration of a selfish or hurtful act makes its enactment more likely. Temptation may involve the emotional parts of your brain, especially the pleasure center, in a mud-wrestling match with the rational, consequences-aware work of the cortex. Perhaps you can avoid being led into temptation by limiting the content of your imagination.

Spiritual Disciplines

Another aphorism from brain science seems to apply to repeated, ritualistic practices of the faith: "Neurons that fire together, wire together." In ritual, the brain creates habituated responses, which are the most efficient ways by which humans encounter the vast majority of life's circumstances. Habits are formed when repeated actions are interpreted by mindful reflection.

Spiritual disciplines (such as prayer, regularized worship, financial generosity, home devotions, Bible reading, repetitions of spiritual sayings, and ritualized movement) can become the preferred responses—or default actions—of the human brain at times of need.

Trying It Out

Use a Greek or Hebrew lexicon or concordance to find shades of meaning for *mind* or *thought*. Check the cited references to see how your knowledge of brain science might add just a little twist or spark to familiar Bible passages.

One other note about developing spiritual disciplines. The brain learns best by doing. Another brain maxim summarizes this truth: "You act your way into thinking." This suggests that in order to become more spiritual, you might begin by engaging in spiritually mature actions without waiting for your attitudes to mature. Spiritual discipline first comes from activity, and from thoughtfulness about the action.

Finding the Brain in the Bible

The Bible was not written to provide good copy for a twenty-first century book on brain science and the church, even though that would have made writing this chapter much simpler! The Bible was written to lead you to know and love your God, and to reveal Christ as Word of God. Because knowing God certainly involves appreciating God's creating Spirit, you can read the Scriptures with the expectation that you will find reasons for awe-filled worship of God.

With those benefits of God's revelation firmly in mind, you can look at some parts of the Scriptures with a brain science filter, engaging in a different kind of exegetical enterprise. Follow me while I try that idea on a few passages and stories of Scripture and see if any new ideas jump out at you.

The Fall (Genesis 3)

Adam and Eve commit the first sin, wanting to be gods and to have all knowledge. They—and their hapless descendants at the Tower of Babel—are punished for wanting to overload their brains with knowledge, mistaking it for power. On the face of it, the actions of our first ancestors are both deplorable (there is only one God) and stupid (the human brain can handle only so much information at one time). For brain scientists this story embodies the difficult question of whether human brains are hardwired for good or evil. For those of us easily embarrassed, the story shows how our human family didn't get a very good start on "smart."

The Great Shema (Deuteronomy 6:5)

In this statement, which is foundational to both Judaism and Christianity, humans are enjoined to love God with their minds, a concept that reaches back into the most ancient of times. Repeated several times in both testaments, this important precept illustrates the Jewish and early Christian belief that mind and soul belonged to God and were best

directed to God's service. A cautionary note: because the physical importance of *brain* was not known until centuries after the scriptures were
written, the Bible does not deal with the relationship of *mind* and *brain*.

Gideon and the Midianites (Judges 6–8)

The camel-riding, fearsome, marauding Midianites are defeated by
a ragtag army of Israelites who use fear as their primary weapon. "Stress
makes people stupid" is evident as the Midianites flee and fight (with
each other). God triumphs with a few courageous brains.

Sharpened Wits (Proverbs 27:17)

Iron does sharpen iron, just as conversations and admonitions
among other people sharpen minds, faces, or wits, depending on the
translation you use for this verse. Brain science has shown the value of
conversation in drawing people together for common purposes, sooth-
ing stressed minds and allowing love to enter relationships. (Want to try
a challenge? Rename all your meetings as conversations, using conversational styles of interaction and see what changes.)

Out of the Heart (Matthew 15:18-19)

The mind (in some versions,
"the heart") is the source of everything that comes out of the
mouth, and the source of evil
actions. "What you can imagine,
you can do" applies here. Why?
The same neuronal circuits that
are involved in imagining a physical act are also active in actually
carrying out that act. So when you
imagine dark thoughts about cell

Brain Fact

Your heart supplies your brain with
all its nutrients. Although your brain
comprises only 2 percent of your
body's mass, it uses 20 percent of all
your body's nutrient energy. Brain
imaging technology measures patterns of blood flow as your brain
works.

phone users in crowded restaurants, don't be surprised with the destructive words that come out of your mouth!

Paul's "Wretched Man" (Romans 7:14-25)

Paul writes about this sorry state, his lack of integrity when his intentions and his actions don't match. What's going on might be that two parts of Paul's brain—the reptilian and mammalian—are having a brain custody battle with his cortex.

The Mind of Christ (Philippians 2:5-8)

Paul encourages an attitude of selfless altruism that is modeled on Jesus' own temperament. Jesus' purposeful emptying out accomplishes a greater good. Jesus' state of mind is focused on a singular sense of his lifework. Can the same state of mind be possible for you, whose brain is just as human as Jesus' own?

Thinking on Things (Philippians 4:8)

"Think about whatever is good!" summarizes this admonition from Paul. It's also a good piece of advice about which thoughts—and their connected actions—are preferable habits in the brains of Christians. If nutritionists and brain scientists constructed a unified axiom for all of life, it might read, "You are what you eat and you do what you think."

Looking at the Bible with the Brain in Mind

Try the following suggestions when you use a brain-based hermeneutic with Scripture:

- Don't retrofit contemporary brain science onto Scripture or its characters. The writers and the storytellers understood little of the workings of the human brain. Even the idea of *mind* may not have had the same meaning for Old and New Testament writers as it does for us today.
- At the same time, the human brain probably hasn't changed much over the last six to ten thousand years, which makes it fair to ask the

simple question, "What might have been occurring in the brains of the individuals in this story or passage?"

- "God's mind" is an inadequate metaphor, even though it may be necessary at times. God is always "totally Other," and so ascribing a human mind to God always minimizes God's full nature. Human brains are finite in their capacity and in the work they can do. God is not limited, in any way.

- In applying Scripture to your life, ask yourself brain-based questions, such as "How do you know such-and-such is true?" "How does this truth from God change my mind?" "What in this passage brings relief, order, integrity, hope to my troubled state of mind?" "What's good for my brain here?" and "If I accept this ideal, how would my thinking and acting be different?"

Some Difficulties Remain

If theology and brain science can embrace, then they can also get on each other's nerves. Like odd-coupled roommates, both bodies of knowledge struggle for recognition in a world increasingly overloaded with information. Problems remain or could arise between them.

Elusive Proof

Proof, at least empirically verifiable truth, eludes both brain science and theology. Neurobiological fact can easily get lost in reductionistic minutia, and theological truth can sometimes defy measurement. Scientists and theologians might easily name each other's limitations without seeing their own shortcomings, thus reducing cooperative venturing and conjecturing.

Renewed Antagonism

The history of the relationship between science and theology is fraught (Don't you just love the sound of that word?) with long periods of conflict. In recent history, evolutionists and creationists have added rancor to the relationship between science and religion, yielding a continuing mistrust that could easily spill over into the relationship between theology and neuroscience. And that would be more fraught than any of our brains would want to handle!

Turf Wars

As you've probably gathered in your reading here, brain science and theology lay claim to many of the same conceptual and emotional territories. Inevitably, there will be places where those claims conflict with each other and where tensions will grow. For example, theology and brain science may eventually disagree about sin—its nature, causes, and effects. (Several decades ago, *alcoholism* was viewed as a sin, then was redefined as "sickness," and now is perhaps most accurately described neurobiologically as an "expressed genetic predisposition.")

Moralizing Neurobiology

Highly purposed church leaders may press brain science to reckon with (or explain) vexing problems in the world, such as injustice, sexism, classism, or violence. Brain scientists may resist applying their work to moral issues.

Amoral Brain Science

On the other hand, without ethical underpinnings, neuroscience could easily be pressed into the service of oppression or injustice. (Hitler's horrific actions were, in his mind, justified by carefully chosen elements of science.) Theology can help neuroscience hold to its historically ethical foundations.

New Hermeneutics

At some point, a more mature neurobiology may be incorporated into yet-to-be-developed methods of biblical interpretation. Just as historical-critical methods or literary criticism revolutionized the interpretation of Scripture, so brain science might invite us to move beyond present methods of exegesis. If you already know about *neurotheology*, and *nueroeconomics* shows up on Web browsers, can *neurohermeneutics* or *neurosermons* be far behind?

Much More to Think About

In this chapter I've explored the connections between two fields of human endeavor. Because the look was only a glance, you may want to read further in the field of neurotheology, especially as it develops over the next several years. Remember to approach what you read with discernment and to be prepared to be amazed at God's handwriting in both arenas of human thought. That's always a good way to approach the God who created your brain!

Looking Ahead

In the next few chapters I'll examine how brain science affects the life of congregations, its leaders and its members. To keep things simple, I've chosen a few well-established areas of brain science to explore: growth and development, foreground and background, danger and opportunity, and learning and memory. My intent is to help you see how normal activities of the human brain play out in the normal—and sometimes not-so-normal—behaviors and structures of congregations.

In chapter 2, I'll start with the subject of growth and development, and then consider the application of cell birth, neuroplasticity, and cell death to congregational dynamics. By the end of the chapter, you'll also understand what all those terms mean. Get ready for what you'll be reading by thinking about the following statement: life depends on death.

Exploring Further

With a small group of people, examine any of the following questions or try some of the suggested activities. Make up your own follow-up activities to personalize what you've read.

1. Search for *neurotheology* on your Web browser and see what comes up. Before you read uncritically, assess the sources of the information for their scientific objectivity and credibility, their obvious or hidden purposes, and their associations with organizations or efforts already known to you. Check several Web sites for similarities, patterns, or clues about other places to investigate.

2. Revisit some of the places in this chapter where your "Aha!" moments were colored with excitement, high curiosity, or even a little fear. Talk about the reasons for those feelings, and ask others for their reactions. For example, how do you feel about the fact that we can now watch "brains at prayer" on scanning machines?

3. Based on what you've read, what do you see as the greatest opportunity for the church as it incorporates neuroscience into its theology?

4. From your other reading on the subject, what was not covered well in this chapter? Where might you go to find more information or wisdom on the topic?

5. Find a current brain-focused article from a newspaper, newsmagazine, or scientific journal and talk with someone else about the possible theological connections or implications of what you have read.

Chapter 2

Connecting the Dots

Growth and Development

WHEN I WAS A CHILD, one of my favorite activities in school was completing connect-the-dot pictures. On the page in front of me would be scores of numbered dots, with the implied invitation to connect the dots to make a picture. Being a precocious dot-connector, of course, I connected the dots to form pictures of the signing of the Augsburg Confession, the ever-popular Katie Luther making beer, and J. S. Bach tuning his clavichord. (Did I mention the part about this being a Lutheran day school?) The activity was fun—when the dots were connected—but also challenging because the picture was not completely evident until all of the numerals were linked.

Other people know the joy and power of dot-connecting, too. Author, consultant, and community developer Luther Snow (*The Power of Asset Mapping*, Alban Institute, 2004) talks about the value of connecting the dots in planning processes. For Snow, dot-connecting is the place where growth and development take place, where God's grace makes a cohesive whole out of seemingly disconnected dots—assets or gifts.

In this chapter I will link together a collection of brain science dots to fashion a picture titled, "The Growth and Development of Your Brain and Your Congregation." Although the idea-picture hasn't been given a formal biological or ecclesiastical designation, three of its functions have well-understood names:

1. Cell growth and regeneration—the ways in which the human brain puts new cells where none recently existed. (The ways in which congregations are formed and transformed.)
2. Neuroplasticity—the ability of brain cells, individually and in neuronal bundles, to change functions quickly. (The ability of congregations to adjust to changing times, changing visions, and changing membership.)
3. Cell death—why and how your brain gets rid of its own cells, starting before birth. (Why and how congregations eventually die, even before they're born.)

After I've explored each of these three elements in the brain, I'll suggest how they might apply to congregations. But first, let's look together at the big idea of growth and development.

Big Picture: Growth and Development

The life cycles of all living things include the elements of birth, growth and development, and death. Your body is no different. After a period of gestation, you are born—an inexact term if it's taken to mean "becoming alive." Your body develops over time, changing and growing larger and more complex. Eventually, when one or more of your body's constitutive mechanisms have grown and developed past the point of sustainability, they shut down and you die.

Because they are living organisms, your brain and your congregation are also born, grow and develop, and die. The key functions of all organisms are similar across the spectrum of living things. To begin and sustain their lives, organisms display essentially similar behaviors, forms, and functions. The principles are simple:

1. Growth involves a measurable increase in size or weight.
2. Development involves the addition or modification of your body's structures.

3. What's true about the smallest organism is most likely also true of the largest organism.
4. What's true of an organism might also be functionally true of its constitutive parts.
5. What's true of individual organisms is most likely true of collections of organisms, such as herds, colonies, families, or congregations.

Some examples may help. A single neuron in your brain has similar functions (input–processing–output) as the entire brain, with functions similar to those of a congregation. Movement shows up in cell development, your brain, and your congregation. (See chapter 5 for a review of these ideas.)

What's true of a single brain is also true of a room full of brains. So when you speak about how your brain forms, grows, develops, and dies, you could also be speaking about your congregation's life cycle. Some examples include the following:

- A brain adds cells before the fully developed fetus is born, and yet-to-be-chartered congregations add members before the official date of their institutional formation.
- In order to grow, a brain needs nutrients. A congregation needs the rich food of God's Word and Sacrament to grow into mature service to God.
- Brain cells readily change functions to meet changing conditions. Congregation members (especially leaders like you) change roles, offices, and tasks in order to maintain stability and vitality in the face of changing contexts or changing purposes.
- The skull houses your brain so that it can carry out its functions well. The church building houses the people of God assembled together for common purpose.
- Your brain is literally rejuvenated—youthful vigor is restored—as some brain cells die and others regenerate themselves. Your congregation renews itself as new members join your fellowship *and* as present members regain excitement and energy for their role as stewards of God's mysteries.

Let's turn now to the exploration of three specific phenomena to see how growth and development occur in your brain and in your congregation.

Cell Growth and Regeneration in Your Brain

In the not-too-distant past, the conventional wisdom was that your brain's deck of cards was dealt to you at birth. "You have all the brain cells you will ever have, so don't be stupid about their care and feeding" was one way some folks talked about brain development.

During the past several years, however, brain scientists have discovered that the matter is much more complex, and much more hopeful. As they have studied cell growth and regeneration, they have encountered new features and capacities of the human brain to restore itself. The following examples illustrate that emerging body of research.

News Cells at Any Age

Because of their research on single neurons, scientists now know that brain cells can regenerate no matter how old a person might be. Cell generativity is determined by growth factors, chemical compounds secreted into the human brain. New cells grow and develop when nerve growth factor (NGF), fibroblast growth factor (FGF), insulin growth factor (IGF), or tumor growth factor (TGF) are present in exact amounts required by the brain. Another correlated finding is that cells in aging brains do not die simply because of their age.

Support Cells

Glial (GLEE-uhl) cells help embryonic brain cells migrate. In your adult brain they surround and consume dying neurons and insulate healthy neurons so that they can fire efficiently. Brain researchers don't yet know as much about the various kinds of glial cells as they do about neurons. The sheer volume of these cells—there are more than 1 trillion glial cells compared to 100 billion neurons—suggests that they are profoundly necessary for as-yet-unknown functions of your brain. Recent research seems to indicate that glial cells may form separate-but-parallel networks similar to neuronal bundles, and that glial cells may communicate chemically with each other and with neurons. With new imaging techniques, neuroscientists can now detect minute amounts of calcium and adenosine triphosphate (ATP) molecules involved in glial cell function. Research with glial cells will be directed at their involvement with learning, memory formation, and nerve damage repair.

* * *

One practical application: Long after the embryonic stage of life, brain cells retain their capacity to migrate or grow into areas of the brain. This discovery has within the past decade yielded a dependable practical application—Constraint-induced movement (CI) therapy for stroke victims, or those recovering from limb amputation. In this form of physical therapy, movement of the good limb is severely limited, and the damaged limb is forced to engage in repetitive movement until nearly complete function is restored. This cortical reorganization (or remapping) may also be useful in other matters such as memory loss, learning methods, or recovery from spinal cord injuries.

> **Brain Fact**
>
> Why is it hard to learn a second language later in life? Your brain has to grow new connections so that the phonemes of the second language don't compete for the attention of brain cells already dedicated to the phonemes of your primary language.

It may seem self-evident that your brain could have the same capacity for regeneration as your skin, hair, or fingernails. On the other hand, for centuries we have accepted the notion that the process of dying begins when your brain inevitably runs out of viable neurons. We now know that the human brain can grow new cells and send them to new places for new or renewed functions. New questions require new answers. Some are disturbing, some are promising, and some defy label:

- What's the relationship between the too-rapid cell growth of cancers and your brain's ability to regenerate itself?

- What is a natural death?
- What causes of death can be diminished or delayed?
- How might you rethink the definition of a normal life span? (Some scientists conjecture that normal human life expectancy might extend 150 years.)
- How should you change your attitudes about the elderly?
- In what ways are you in control of your own destiny? In what ways are you not?

Cell Growth and Regeneration in Your Congregation

At one time, it was considered normal that a congregation would work only with the members it had been given, carefully shepherding a limited number of families (with the same demographic profile) through several generations. In these times, however, church leaders of almost every stripe have come to see that the lasting vitality of congregations is more likely ensured when they grow more diverse, not only racially or ethnically but also in other demographic categories.

These new elements that contribute to a congregation's continued liveliness are most likely not available to a congregation by virtue of some kind of denominational or locational genetics. In the past, for example, middle-class Lutherans moving to suburban Los Angeles would most likely join a congregation of middle-class Lutherans located in that same suburb. In these times, however, the brain cells of potential congregational members can migrate from anywhere to anywhere, transforming the shape and direction of any congregation.

Just as the brain can grow new cells at any age, so also with congregations-as-brains. However elderly a congregation might be, its individual members can take on new energy, grow into new places (or roles) in the congregation's life, or combine with other members to take on new ministries. Neighborhoods regentrify and change racial composition, economic factors change, and new pastors and leaders arise.

Just like the brain depends on a variety of growth factors to renew itself, congregations benefit from small-but-significant events, resources, or experiences that provide leaders renewed energy, excitement, and skill for their ministries.

Glial cells have their analogues in congregations. Glial cells function as a separate network of brain cells to support the brain, sometimes in unknown or invisible ways. In congregations, glial cells might correspond to unknown and invisible networks of members who work quietly to support you as a leader—in prayer, for example—or whose unnamed ministries in your congregation undergird its visible institutional life. (Consider, for example, the knots of conversation at the end of a worship service, where care and comfort are extended, ideas generated, gratitude expressed.)

Neuroplasticity in Your Brain

You already see how to take apart the word, right?

- *Neuro*—having to do with neurons, the brain cells that fire in chains and bundles of synapses.
- *Plasticity*—the capacity of a substance to be shaped into different forms in order to fulfill different functions, and to retain each form and function until the next change comes around. (Like a new kind of claydough that can be shaped and also shape itself!)

So *neuroplasticity* refers to the ability of bundles of nerve cells— mostly the cells related to the cortex (the thinking brain)—to change their functions within milliseconds in response to changes in their environment, or in anticipation of those changes. Individual cells have the same capacity, but it's easier to see forms and functions when we talk about bundles—interrelated groups of cells that seem to work together for specific tasks.

Neuroplasticity means that the brain is *not* composed entirely of little packages of cells with team jerseys and numbers like "Neuron Bundle #46,680: Nice Words Receiver" or "Neuron Circuit #43,004: Letter 'N' Halfback." Discreet brain bunches are not waiting on some mental football bench for the right stimulus to call them into the game with other well-labeled team members. Instead, most areas of your brain have the ability to use and reuse cell bundles in a variety of configurations for a variety of functions. Some brain areas—especially subcortical regions—are modular, dedicated to specific functions.

How does your brain gain this capability? There isn't much credible defense any more for views that your brain's abilities—including plasticity—are determined primarily by nature or nurture. Those two extremes can be characterized the following way:

Brain Fact

In his new synthesis of neural Darwinism, *Wider Than the Sky: The Phenomenal Gift of Consciousness*, Nobel Laureate Gerald Edelman explores the idea of *degeneracy*. In common use, the term connotes deterioration, but in biology and in physics degeneracy is the capacity of an organism or physical entity to take on different and discrete forms or states in order to yield the same function or result.

- Primarily nature: neuronal activity happens because of genetic absolutes. (Your deck of cards is already shuffled and ready to be dealt out; you don't get any more cards.)
- Primarily nurture. (Because at birth "your mind is a blank slate," its capabilities are formed by the environment in which it lives.)

Instead of holding these absolutist positions, most brain scientists now see the matter as a wonderfully complex interplay between these two shaping forces. Your brain shapes and is shaped by both its environment and its genetic predispositions. Both are fundamental to the brain's development. Neuroplasticity occurs in the following ways.

Cell Migration

As the human brain develops *in utero,* brain cells migrate (or grow toward) the areas of the brain where they will eventually settle. Organized growth in brain cells occurs until about age 25, when the adult brain seems to be fully formed.

Hardwiring

Because of repeated use following genetically determined predispositions, groups of brain cells in a normal adult brain develop preferred patterns of firing that become "hardwired." Another way of saying, "Cells that fire together wire together."

Multifunctionality

Most of these cell groups can switch among several different functions, sometimes within milliseconds of each other. For example, the same bundle of millions of cells has the capacity to both imagine and execute a specific behavior. "Act your way into thinking" and "What you can imagine you can do" both describe neuroplasticity. Or, the neuronal pathway involved in religious ecstasy is also active in sexual orgasm.

Circuit-Washing

In the microseconds it takes brain circuits (connected bundles of brain cells) to switch among functions, the brain chemically cleans away the previous synapse's arrangement of chemicals. This prepares that circuit for its next task, the reorganizing of those same chemicals for another function. This circuit-washing and rearrangement take just a little longer when your brain is confronted with surprising or "Aha!" moments.

Personal Epiphanies

Your capacity for sudden insight—as in "*Now* I understand why only bald men enjoy making the sign of the cross on top of their heads!"—is evidence of neuroplasticity. Another way to talk about this phenomenon is to say that new brain connections are being formed where none had existed before.

Cell Growth and Death

Your brain maintains its neuronal flexibility because it can both create new cells and destroy unwanted cells. (We'll say more about this later in the chapter.)

Brain Repair

If your brain is damaged or altered in some way—for example, in strokes, brain-damaging accidents, or diseases—the cells of your brain have the potential for *cross-modal reassignment,* which means brain cells grow (or migrate) toward empty or dead areas of your brain and take up the functions of the cells previously occupying that space. (Recall the earlier description of constraint-induced movement therapy.)

* * *

Neuroplasticity may seem like just another way to talk about how any part of the body constantly adjusts to its context. Because it's part of the body, your brain is no less capable than, say, fingers that can turn the pages of this book and seconds later grasp the handle of that cup of hot peppermint tea you've been savoring.

Brain Fact

In the United States, about 600,000 people suffer strokes each year. That works out to be about one victim every 52 seconds. The majority—about 440,000—don't die immediately. Of that number, about 300,000 suffer serious disabilities.

When you look at neuroplasticity a little more closely, the questions and answers get more complex. The subject also gets more frangible: When asked and answered, questions about neuroplasticity fragment into thousands of little questionettes, each as fascinating to consider as the original. Some examples include the following:

• What activates a specific bundle of brain cells to fire in one way and not another? It's not the genes. There aren't enough genes to assign each one to control a specific synapse. The numbers don't add up;

the approximately 30,000 genes in the human genome cannot individually connect to cells in the human brain, which outnumber
genes many times over. Some other deeper, quieter mechanism compels the alignment of the chemical compounds that are involved in
cell firing patterns.

- Are all parts of your brain capable of change, even those hardwired
  in the brain stem or limbic (emotional) areas?
- Could your brain's capacity to reassign cells to new functions indicate an unlimited human potential for cell repair or regeneration?
- Is learning simply a matter of training brain cells—through repeated
  experiences such as drills and rote learning—so that they grow into
  certain areas of your brain? Can it be better defined as "increasing
  the brain's ability to assign multiple functions to bundles of cells?"
  (See chapter 5 for additional ideas about learning and memory.)

Neuroplasticity in Your Congregation

Your brain's flexibility in functioning corresponds to many of the
best features of your congregation-as-brain. What a wonderful gift from
God! (Think what your congregation would be like if each member—
and your pastor—was capable of only one wonderful role or task, or had
only one narrowly directed set of gifts.) Follow me for a few paragraphs
as I outline some congregational dynamics that correspond to your
brain's plasticity (or degeneracy).

One of the most exhilarating qualities of healthy congregations is
the way bundles of members (like bundles of neurons) come together
for specific tasks, go about their business and then regather at a later
time to take on another responsibility. In your congregation, these neuronal bundles could be women's circles, men's groups, committees, small
groups, informal coffee klatches, the after-choir-rehearsal bar-visiting
group, parents of toddlers, or the affinity groups that form around special projects or events. These groups communicate within their relationships by simple conversation. They assess their capacities, then find and
fill needs that match those assets.

How do members of your congregation—its neurons—acquire
their capacity? Some members have the requisite ideals, attitudes,

knowledge, and skill almost by virtue of their genetic predispositions. They are parts of families or long-standing relationships in which those capacities are formed, nourished, and rewarded over generations. Other members acquire flexible capacities for ministry by virtue of their exposure to your congregation's shaping influences: ministry of Word and Sacrament, programs, activities, friendships, and the love and care they experience within your congregation. Sometimes these congregational neurons are new Christians or new members; sometimes they are long-standing leaders who have been reenergized. In both cases, most likely nature and nurture played roles in forming these individuals into willing and capable servants of Christ.

In your congregation-as-brain, cells that fire together, wire together. Members filled with courage, trust, love, care, and admiration fire over and over again; these actions eventually express themselves as a kind of hardwiring seen in long-standing, sturdy relationships. Conversely (and sadly), members filled with fear, suspicion, anger, selfishness, or jealousy also fire and wire together, forming networks of dysfunctional congregational neurons that are toxic to your congregation's health or vitality.

Circuit-washing in your congregation might be as simple as the capacity of congregation members to forgive each other. The brain chemicals of fear and anger dissipate and are replaced with feel-good congregational neurotransmitters such as joy, shared mission, honor, appreciation, and humor.

How does your congregation repair its neurons? In your congregation, that function might be seen in the willingness of individual members to engage in a kind of cross-modal migration, in which individuals pick up others' dropped balls, missed deadlines, unfinished assignments, or otherwise compensate for underwhelming talent or skill. "The strong" bear the infirmities of "the weak" (Rom. 15:1), expecting that the situation may reverse itself at some future moment.

Cell Death in Your Brain

Cell death might at first seem like a dark subject, perhaps because of our overall fear of death. In reality, however, the mechanisms and effects of cell death may be necessary for your brain to function efficiently throughout life.

The causes of cell death are fascinating. Because of both internal and external factors—the physical environment, your brain's relationship with other parts of your body, continued stress, idleness—delicate relationships among your brain's systems become unbalanced, resulting in chemical changes that favor some cells and not others. For the human brain to remain alive, there must be a balance between the synthesis and decomposition of brain chemicals. Dying brain cells help maintain that balance, similar to the equilibrium necessary for other ecosystems in nature to survive over long periods of time.

We use the phrase "use it or lose it" to talk about how we lose physical strength or agility. That aphorism also characterizes one cause of cell death, synaptic weakening. Synaptic weakening occurs when neurons are idle. The strength and viability of synapses decrease due to the diminished presence of vital chemicals—such as calcium—or some of the more than 60 identified neurotransmitters. Neurotransmitters are chemical compounds that work throughout the body—like glutamate, dompamine, serotonin, endorphins, and oxytocin—and in the brain help synapses to fire efficiently. You could think of them as chemical messengers between brain cells. Because of your brain's efficiency in its use of limited chemical resources, cells that are idle don't need the chemicals, and the chemicals are used by other cells. Another way of thinking about the matter—and a metaphor found only in this book—"Couch potatoes (cells) are cooked and eaten."

Brain cells can also die if they experience too much of a good thing. For example, neurons can be excited to death by the excess of glutamate, a chemical necessary for normal synapse functioning. Termed *excitotoxicity*, this overabundance of a normally beneficial chemical is a central feature of strokes, paralysis, epilepsy, and dementia. Excess amounts of oxygen, calcium, monosodium glutamate (MSG), and several amino acids may also contribute to cell death.

Not all cell death is accidental, nor should we presume that cell death is always a negative event in the human brain. Cell death is necessary for your brain to thrive. In programmed cell death—sometimes called cell suicide—your brain purposefully deprives large numbers of brain cells of needed nutrients, and thus they die. These cell deaths are a kind of "pruning," in which nonuseful cells are removed so that the remaining cells can function well. This process begins as early as the eighth month of pregnancy, when the fetus sloughs off about half of its brain cells. This pruning occurs at other times in human development—during the later years of adolescence—and doesn't seem to be complete until adulthood.

Programmed cell death has been given another name, *apoptosis*, derived from the Greek term for the necessary loss of leaves on a tree. Apoptosis is similar to other cyclical biological phenomena in which seeming death makes life possible. Caterpillars die inside cocoons and emerge as butterflies. Seeds dry into death before their embryos spring to life again, feeding on the stored energy in their endosperms. So brain cells that die leave room for brain cells that live. Chemicals from the dead cells—especially nerve growth factor—are available for the benefit of living cells. With fewer cells in a given area of your brain, the remaining cells connect to each other more slowly but also more efficiently because they are working at full potential. A similar occurrence: in a not-so-crowded restaurant, your server has further to walk between customers, but each one gets really good service.

The matter of cell death, especially programmed cell death (or cell suicide), gives rise to any number of tantalizing conceptual and ethical questions, including the following:

- If your brain allows (or causes) cells to die for the good of the rest of the brain, what might that mean for other forms of purposeful death, such as assisted suicide?
- What will happen when the causes for cell death are well understood and it becomes possible to delay or eliminate it?
- If you interrupt the patterns of programmed cell death, will your brain become less or more capable?
- To whom—and for what reasons—will cures for brain disease or mental illness first become available?
- How should you view the entire concept of death?

Cell Death in Your Congregation

At first glance, the subject of cell death in your congregation seems like a morbid, anxiety-producing matter. Individual members of your congregation (its neurons, remember?) get older and eventually die, and when enough of these neurons have died, the congregation-as-brain dies as well. Along the path of growth and development toward that inevitable end, the brains of many congregations start to fill with fear of institutional death.

As with your own brain, cell death in your congregation is not always a fearful or harmful thing. In fact, it may be an important and necessary attribute of your congregation that some of its members leave the congregation. Periodic roll cleaning, a kind of programmed cell death, removes members (neurons) who are no longer active or no longer taking advantage of the neurotransmitters of your congregation, such as worship, education, fellowship, or service. Even the deaths of beloved members may eventually prove beneficial to a congregation's long-term vitality. (An easy example is an individual who deeply loves your congregation, and provides for a mission endowment that expands the scope of your congregation's service to people who are poor. A more difficult example might be the death of an extremely active member that creates both the need and the space for other, newer members' assets and energies.)

A troubling kind of cell death in your congregation can be the slow lapse of once-active members into a state of institutional inactivity. In small increments—whether by their own choice or because they have been ignored—these individuals are deprived of essential spiritual nutrients, and slowly strangle or starve to death, spiritually and relationally. The continuing detachment of some members from the activities of your congregation could result in the congregational version of synaptic weakening. Members who are absent or idle are not likely to participate in the neuronal synapses of your congregation's life—conversations, personal witnessing, times of devotion and prayer—and thus gradually lose their spiritual strength and vitality.

Another kind of cell death in congregations has bothered me for years, a phenomenon I have experienced several times, sometimes as a contributing cause: the burn out of lively congregational neurons who are too busy, too active, too involved, too dependent on the congregation's neurotransmitters. "Too much of a good thing" describes their spiritual lives, as does the phrase, "He/she practically lives down at church!" The exitotoxicity these individuals experience is precisely the opposite from the condition of individuals who gradually drop out of the congregation because they are deprived of spiritual nutrients. In this case, an excess of congregational glutamate—too many friends, too many noble purposes, or too strong of a desire to care for others—gradually builds up in these congregational neurons. What would otherwise be good becomes toxic in overabundant quantities, and these formerly faithful leaders suddenly drop away from the church's life. In some cases, their spiritual center dies as well.

In spite of cell death—or perhaps because of it—congregations continue as viable places where God's people are equipped. Just as your brain takes advantage of the seemingly somber circumstance of cell death, so, too, your congregation-as-brain can benefit from the constant pruning process of cell death, and can remain strong in spite of its losses. From personal experience, your brain knows this is true.

Connecting the Dots in Earnest

Let's try to see what we can learn from cell growth and regeneration, neuroplasticity and cell death when we draw some lines between them.

Interconnectedness

First, the three brain processes are related to each other in the following ways:

- Cell growth and cell death both occur in the presence of the same chemicals, although the chemicals are present in differing combinations and differing amounts. (The people, programs, and preaching of your congregation can cause both spiritual growth and death.)
- Each of the three processes may cause the other. Neuroplasticity would not be possible if the brain was clogged with dead or nonfunctioning cells. Cell growth and migration may be necessary for your brain to engage in thousands of tiny repairs. If there are no new cells, your brain loses some of its plasticity. (In your congregation, it's always hard to distinguish cause from effect. Perhaps it's enough just to know that everything connects.)

Fundamental Processes or Functions

Taken together, these three functions may constitute the way human organs and tissues are formed. Cell growth and migration in the embryonic brain enable it to begin assuming control of the fetus's development. Absent these three features of your brain, it's likely that vital functions—emotion, thought, consciousness—would be static or limited, or that your brain would inevitably deteriorate. (As you evaluate the qualities that make up your

Brain Fact

Neurons transmit information through a kind of electrochemical chitchat among cells. Information takes the form of electrical signals that are generated by positively charged potassium and sodium ions, or negatively charged calcium ions.

congregation, remember to think about all three of these metaphoric characteristics as necessary ingredients for your congregation's life.)

Big Question

If neuroplasticity is an early and lingering capability of the human brain, does this mean that we all began life with brains like a blank slate? Another way of stating the question might be, "Is there any capability or quality of the human brain that's innate and essentially unchangeable? Why or why not?"

Brain Growth and Development Outside the Church

As brain growth and development becomes better understood, it will become more significant for daily living. For example, the mechanisms of neuroplasticity—especially the matter of cross-modal reassignment we visited earlier in this chapter—have already become important keys to the treatment of strokes, Lou Gehrig's disease, Alzheimer's, trauma, and epilepsy. Prenatal health care becomes more crucial because we now know that critical stages in the human brain's development occur well before birth.

For several decades, several helpful models of learning have been based on the developing evidence of brain science. How children think, how they learn to read, how they respond to classroom discipline—all now routinely reference brain science as verification or proof of the efficacy of a particular approach or theory. As a newly understood function of the human brain, neuroplasticity might support either highly structured rote learning or discovery-based methodologies. Research into the timing of spurts in brain cell growth (and death) may soon determine the effectiveness of instructional strategies that direct or shape children's character development or emotional intelligence. Eventually, some social critics will hook together cause-and-effect relationships between these three brain processes and such cultural artifacts as television viewing, diet, stress, the ideal workplace, or subtle humor in books about brain science and the church.

Brain Fact

Dopamine (DOPE-uh-meen) has been called the learning neurotransmitter because it links reward sensations and long-term memory. Dopamine also carries out two balancing functions: it makes neurons more ready to fire while decreasing the spontaneous firing of neurons.

Bonus Section

Practical Applications in Congregations

THE FOLLOWING PAGES suggest places where neuroplasticity, cell growth and regeneration, and cell death could be important to specific ministries in your congregation.

Youth Ministry

However you view teens—in ministry with adults, as the objects of ministry, or as late-night refrigerator emptiers—you have to reckon with the reality that teen brains won't be fully developed until about age 25. At some point in later adolescence, teens go through stages of rapid cell growth and rapid cell death. Those are hardly times of settled, solid thought processes, and may not be the most opportune times for adults to think of teens as equal partners. (They are times to keep your pantry and refrigerator well stocked, if at all possible.)

On the other hand, these may be the last times when developing brains are most open to reorganization (or remapping of reality). The best way to take advantage of this stage in life may be to challenge youth with focused experiences—encounters with persons who are poor, conversations with elderly members, career-discerning retreats—and spiritually deep questions. You might ask yourself some pertinent questions: How could teens become familiar with people and ideas different from their own? How could their assumptions about their present or future lifestyles be challenged beyond "We will live forever, starting today"?

Adolescent brains still need careful accompaniment through the final stages of brain growth. Teens need care and forgiveness. Research into the brain's need for and response to forgiveness suggests that this Christ-like behavior can become a kind of default emotional state of mind. Teens don't need adults who patronize them or pander to their enviable youthfulness.

Try out some of the following musings and questions to bring youth ministry into a brain-based framework:

- How could your congregation help teenagers choose lifestyle elements that support optimal brain cell growth and development—factors such as balanced diet, rest, and frequent exercise—and minimize behaviors that detract from brain growth and health?
- In whom and how easily do youth in your congregation find the necessary wisdom and perspective they need in order to care for their brains for the rest of their lives? For example, who helps teenagers develop social intelligence, self-love, mindfulness, or nonanxious presence?
- What could you do to help parents maintain parental roles and "I'm the adult here" authority, provide brain-enriching environments, and respect the growing independence and self-differentiation of their children?
- How does your congregation help teenagers explore a variety of spiritual interests and develop spiritual disciplines? These two faith practices take advantage of the rapid neuronal growth teens will experience during adolescence.
- How do you provide times of contemplation and neuronal quietude that provide relief from the harried and hurried stresses that tax teen brains?

Pregnancy Ministry

If important neuronal development begins during gestation, your congregation might need to rethink how you assist mothers- and fathers-to-be during this time.

Perhaps one or two members might start a pregnancy ministry that precedes the classic cradle roll. That ministry might include some of the following:

- Standard prenatal education about diet, rest, and at-risk behaviors, but with specific connections to the development of the fetal brain.
- Awareness about the emerging frontiers of prenatal care, including the role of fathers. Could a small group in your congregation assume the task of reading magazine articles or conducting Web searches for current information about this topic?

> **Brain Fact**
>
> Three important phases of rapid cell growth occur during pregnancy, and the fetus prunes half its brain cells between the eighth and ninth month of gestation.

- Special care and accompaniment of mothers-to-be during the final months of pregnancy. For example, how could your congregation reduce at-home or church-related stress during that month? What would you pray about with pregnant women during that time? How could your congregation help expectant mothers and fathers find joy and humor in their ministries of gestation?
- How could you take advantage of the neuroplasticity of brain circuits used both to imagine and carry out actions? For example, how might you use imaging exercises to help pregnant women and spouses prepare for their new roles and responsibilities?

Ministry among Elderly Persons

Much of the impact of brain research in the areas of neuroplasticity, cell regeneration, and cell death has been applied to the field of gerontology. This could be a good thing for your congregation if you're becoming filled with aging boomers and their elders. If that's true, it would make sense for your congregation to apply these three features of brain science in programs, events, or congregational structures. Among the possibilities might be the following:

- "Use it or lose it" suggests that a majority of aging adults can bene-fit from increased challenges—mental and physical stretchings that increase the capacities of minds and bodies. How does that happen in your congregation?
- You might look for places where your congregation needs to confess its misperceptions regarding the brain-based capabilities of older members. How are seniors invisibly patronized, seen as less than able or even considered problematic? How do you automatically accept the stereotype that older members will resist change? How are older adults excluded from important decision-making or goal-set-ting, or their presumed worth relegated to minor roles or tasks?
- Leaders and members of your congregation can advocate among local caregiving or assisted-living facilities for programs and facili-ties that enable growth in elderly residents' brain capacity. Start the process by noticing the number of residents who spend the major-ity of their waking hours watching television!
- Your congregation's ministry to homebound older adults can be reshaped to include much more than pleasant conversation, prayer, and Holy Communion. How might you retrain visiting caregivers so that they bring along humor, current events, stimulating inquiry, and other activities that foster brain cell growth?
- Under the supervision of a parish nurse or other professional staff, congregation volunteers can assist with some aspects of stroke recovery therapy.
- Congregational groups can offer support and up-to-date brain-based information to members whose parents are living with Alzheimer's disease, dementia, or strokes.

Faith Formation

By its nature, faith formation is related to these three brain processes, so your congregation might readily apply brain-based infor-mation to matters such as these:

- How do members learn to identify and speak about their faith, thus strengthening the neuronal bundles that are active in spiritual mat-ters? Could you think of witnessing as brain-development activity?

- The ministries in your congregation that deepen faith practices (such as generosity, prayer, Bible study, and service) might benefit from a brain-based conceptual overlay. In any of these faith practices, how do ritual and repetition enable a kind of wiring together of brain synapses that will become preferred default behaviors or thought patterns? How does that happen for members of all ages?

Trying It Out

List and describe all the rituals in your congregation's life, both formal and informal times of symbolic acts that have prescribed order and meaning for those who are involved. (HINT: Informal rituals may involve fewer people in less public settings; they may also need to be named.) Think how your congregation could strengthen the importance of these acts so that they are embedded in individual and institutional memory.

- How helpful is your congregation to members with infants? For example, what classes or groups are available to parents who want to enable their children's spiritual growth during this time of rapid brain growth? How are these parents accepted or affirmed when they bring their active or playful children to worship services?

General Congregational Activities and Processes

Just for fun here, let's play around with some other ways in which cell growth, neuroplasticity, and cell death might show up in your congregation. Your congregation might engage in some of the following actions:

- What if you put into your vision or mission statements something about "promoting the growth of the brains and bodies of all whom we encounter"? (Okay, you come up with better language!) How would that change the way you develop programs or events, or define pastoral ministries?
- You could start a stroke-recovery support group, and be identified as "the congregation that knows about people's brains."

- If a parish nurse is part of your staff, she might conduct an audit of the food served at congregational events, looking at how brain cell growth is or is not helped by the meals and snacks you serve.
- You might include in the qualifications for prospective leaders their ability to excite and challenge other members' brains, so that neuroplasticity and cell growth are possible.
- When you name and celebrate significant events in the lives of members, include the final month of pregnancy, the first year of life, and the adolescent years. (These are times when brain cell growth and death occur at significantly higher rates than other times in life.) The coming of age to an adult brain at about age 25 might also be included. What rituals, caring practices, or prayers could you create for these life milestones?

Brain Fact

The amino acid *tryptophan* (TRIP-toe-fan) is part of the chemical foundation for serotonin, a neurotransmitter that is involved in feelings of calmness or serenity. Carbohydrates increase brain concentrations of tryptophan.

- Your congregation's programs are most likely characterized by comfort and care. How could you expand the identity of your congregation to "intellectually challenging," "a place to consider difficult questions," or "offering profound experiences"?
- You can change your methods of planning to take advantage of neuroplastic imagining-and-doing techniques. For example, try imagined-scenario planning, in which participants talk about a planned event or program as they see it taking place in their imaginations. Then take the next step: Decide what needs to happen in order to forge an actual program or event from the imagined reality.
- Assess every congregational activity, every purpose statement, and every advertisement about your congregation to name what is frankly boring and thus hardly helpful for brain development.
- Rethink ministries of your congregation that favor only adherence to authority—"following" in the narrowest sense. These approaches might atrophy the brains of mature Christians if brain-challenging actions such as discovery-based learning, mindful risk taking, faithful searching and questioning, or self-differentiation are not required.

- Your congregation's organizational structure and its physical setting can nurture or limit neuroplasticity. Newsletter formats, committee tasks, the congregation's constitution, monthly calendars, settings for meetings, lighting, and sight lines and sound levels during worship—any of these matters can help or hinder the capacity of members' brains to regenerate, reimagine, or restore themselves. It's hard for your brain to be multifunctional when options are extremely limited.
- Think about the congregational activities, events, and relationships that help members whose lives—and brains—are in dire need of repair or restoration. For example, how is God's restorative gift of forgiveness proclaimed and practiced in your congregation? How do members learn how to diminish mind-numbing fear or anxiety?
- Quiet ritual or liturgy may have an important role in matters of cell growth or neuroplasticity. How does your congregation provide soulful rest or sabbath times, during which brains rejuvenate or recover?
- Think about how your congregation's leaders may encourage or discourage brain cell growth, or how they punish or care for those whose brains are in need of repair or regeneration. For example, how do you treat members who are encountering mental illness or facing extreme crises?

Big Question

Can you accept the proposition (or is it only a metaphor?) that your congregation is a kind of brain comprised of all its members? Where does the idea work well? Where does it fall apart?

The Last Dot to Be Connected

Back in my picture-drawing days, a path of sequenced numbers guided my dot-connecting toward its eventual end, when I would draw a line from dot 95 back to dot 1. The last hand-drawn line would thus join the ending of my work with its beginning.

We're at the end of this chapter, but it's also the place where we started together. Your brain and your congregation are biologically predisposed to remain alive and vital for decades. Your brain and your congregation are both eminently capable of surviving and even thriving, despite seemingly contrary circumstances. You can trust the connect-the-dots picture I've drawn in this chapter: God accomplishes God's will through your congregation and your brain.

Looking Ahead

In the next chapter, you and I will have a conversation about another important part of brain science—foreground and background. Attention and inattention will also capture your, uhm, well, your *attention*. Before you flip forward to those pages, get ready for your reading by asking the following questions: In your congregation, who pays attention to you? Who doesn't? Why?

Exploring Further

With a small group of people, examine any of the following questions or try some of the suggested activities. Make up your own follow-up activities or personalize what you read here.

1. Name some "Aha!" moments that occurred during your reading. What bits of knowledge or attitudes were replaced or reinforced? Which of the questions in the chapter sparked your curiosity?
2. Take one of the three brain science processes in this chapter (for example, new cell growth) and try some metaphor making. "In my leadership role, 'new cell growth' is like . . ."
3. What practical applications of neuroplasticity, new cell growth, and cell death were *not* covered in this chapter? What would you imagine those applications to be?
4. Where in the chapter did you want to stop and say, "Wait! Tell me more!" What questions would you ask? Why?
5. Ask a child psychologist, educator, or caregiver for elderly persons to join your group and comment on your discussion and sharing.
6. What parts of this chapter could help you in your daily ministries beyond your congregation?

Chapter 3

No Hablo español

Foreground and Background

I'm a denominational headquarters guy, and I'm supposed to know important things. For example, I should be familiar with Bible passages about living for God's purposes, create and implement good and honorable ways to fund God's mission, and, of course, hear, speak, read, and write Spanish. Yes, that's right. In my mind, a fully equipped church bureaucrat should be fluent in español. For any number of reasons and for a variety of good purposes, facility in Spanish is in these times a valuable capability that should fill some of my brain's language processing areas.

My brain, however, misses that mark. On a good day I can understand only about 20 percent of what Spanish speakers say, and on that same high mental acuity day I can read only about 30 percent of the printed Spanish I see. This becomes a major problem when I work with my Hispanic colleagues, Latinos and Latinas whose bilingual skills run ahead of my monolingual brain. My brain's lingual limitations require these colleagues to engage in laborious circlings-back to translate or otherwise bring Bob, the One Language Guy, up to speed. My inability to interpret and think in Spanish hampers my effectiveness when I am planning, learning, and thinking with Hispanic folks. I don't feel good about this deficiency.

I tell this story not to self-flagellate, but to lead you toward the subject of this chapter: how your brain and your church select what is foreground and what is background. Another way to think about the content of this chapter is the attention mechanisms in your brain and in your church.

Big Picture: Foreground and Background

At any moment, your brain and your congregation face far more stimuli than either can process. Since neither your brain nor your congregation can react to everything they encounter, the most pressing task your brain or congregation faces at any moment is deciding what to attend to (foreground) and what merely to monitor (background). What makes the foreground important is its immediacy—how urgent, novel, or reaction-worthy the matter is. What makes the background important is its sustainability—how basic awareness of the situation at hand can be efficiently maintained over time.

> **Brain Fact**
>
> The autonomic (aw-toe-NAH-mik) system is one part of your brain's background system. The autonomic system regulates the internal systems of the body such as breathing, heartbeat, blood pressure, bladder constriction and contraction, movement of the intestines, and glandular secretions.

Foreground and background depend on each other. Without the ability to relegate some brain activity to the background, your brain would encounter everything as new, and would be required to devote large amounts of neuronal capacity to processing everything that your senses took in. Imagine how if would feel if, while you were reading this page, you also had to consciously attend to your breathing, your digestion, and your heart rate. By placing vast amounts of external and internal sensory input into familiar background territory, your brain operates efficiently and effectively.

It almost goes without saying that without attention (foreground) capabilities, your brain would not be able to ensure the safety, comfort, or health of the brain's home, the body. You would not be a viable organism if your brain's only ability was automatic (background) maintenance of basic systems. Absent the potential to react to unexpected stimuli, your brain would be extremely vulnerable to what we charitably refer to as "the vagaries of human existence" such as angry church council members, suddenly generous benefactors, and people who *really* like you as a leader.

Foreground and Background in My Brain

Let's go back to my not knowing Spanish so you can see how foreground and background work. In my brain, the default setting for language is English; the default setting for my self-identity includes English-fluent. When I hear or see English, it's not all that difficult to maintain an awareness of the ebb and flow of speech or words. It's not difficult to retain my sense of self as an English-capable person.

Most of the time my brain relies on its background functions to process most of the phonemes and nuances of this language. Unless my ears or eyes encounter something unusual—conversation, a spellbinding speaker, words brimming with emotion—my brain doesn't need to devote large amounts of neural activity to what's already well known. So I can sit at my desk, surrounded by the sounds of English coming from other, nearby cubicles, and not have conscious memory of what has clearly been heard by my ears. English sounds have been sent to the background of my brain.

Because I believe being fluent in Spanish is important and feel inadequate about my lack of fluency, though, my brain strains to derive meaning from sounds, facial expressions, and other body language accompanying Spanish words and phrases. My memories of high school Latin—about as close as I ever got to learning Spanish—and my meager vocabulary of several hundred Spanish words are pressed into service. Most of the meaning-making mechanisms of my brain work together to answer urgent and important questions such as "What's going on here?" "What are these interesting individuals trying to say?" and "Who am I in this situation?" In my brain, almost every element of "Spanish situations" is in the foreground, and so my attention is always high at those times. It feels as though my entire forebrain is working to attend to Spanish sounds and words, and the people who speak or write them.

During these times of intense attention, other parts of my brain are monitoring the context surrounding me. Unless my safety or comfort are compromised, other sights and sounds—especially those that are familiar—barely register as important. As part of the background work of my brain, my autonomic system maintains heart rate and blood pressure at useful levels. Digestion and respiration continue normally, as do other life-enhancing mechanisms of my body—smelling, tactile awareness, maintenance of emotional well-being, a sense of safety.

Foreground and Background
in Your Congregation

It's not difficult to transfer this functional understanding of your brain into the workings of your congregation. Like your brain, your congregation can't pay attention to everything that occurs. Your congregation makes foreground and background choices in the same fashion for the same reasons that your brain makes those choices. As a larger organism, your congregation takes advantage of those choices so that it can use its energy efficiently to sustain its vitality.

Sermon preaching and sermon hearing are good examples, first about individual brains and then as metaphor for other congregational activities. In your congregation, the brains of individual hearers vacillate between foreground attention and background monitoring of the preacher's pronouncements. Familiar concepts, platitudes,

Brain Fact

Daydreaming during sermons may actually be a sign of effective preaching. The prompts of words and feelings in a sermon can engage parts of the cortex and limbic structures, inviting the brains of hearers to imagine, respond emotionally and physically, and reintegrate their beliefs and self-identity. Therefore, blank stares might actually be signs of deeply engaged brains!

and stories get monitored, folded into hearers' sense of what's safe and comfortable. What's novel, urgent, or emotionally charged moves to the foreground of hearers' brains, and their attention focuses sharply.

Sermon-giving and sermon-receiving also might be a metaphor for larger functions of your congregation. Foreground and background interactions between preacher and assembled hearers show up in the ways your pastor and leaders relate to each other in meetings, conversations, and other personal encounters. The words and wisdom of long-standing leaders, well-established groups and programs, and awareness of "the way we do things around here" may fade into the background over time. On the other hand, new ideas and activities may catch attention simply because they stand out from among what's already known or well worn. This may explain why Flavor of the Month programs, attention-grabbing leaders, and whiz-bang resources catch hold so quickly among congregational leaders uncomfortable with their perpetual background position in members' brains.

How else does this foreground and background situation occur in your congregation? Familiar faces get overlooked—or barely monitored—by pastors attending to other members who are caught up in urgent—or attention-demanding—life situations. Another, related example: Over time, highly appreciated new members lose their novelty in your congregation. They fade into the background and after a few months or years suddenly come to realize that they are not gathering foreground attention like they did when they first became members. Some of them lose heart, feel neglected, and drop out of congregational life.

Denominational identity is another place where foreground and background concerns can be seen. Leaders in your church body or association work hard to keep their brand-name identity from receding into the background or taken for granted by people like you. You may constantly grapple with whether to pay attention to denominational programs and activities, or to the people who promote them. On the one hand, you may find comfort and safety in the (foreground) attention you receive by being part of these programs. On the other hand, you may take your denominational identity for granted and thus relegate it to the background of your congregation's brain. In that case, you might place in a foreground position other programs or activities you believe might attract more members, more excitement, and more attention.

Your foreground and background choices may come down to your answer to the question, "What's in a name?" (I wonder how many years it will take for currently novel names for congregations—for example, "Joy," Spirit in/of the ____," "Hosanna," or "New Life/Joy/Hope/Spirit" variations—to fade into the background. I can imagine that in a few years we might start to see congregation names such as "First Avenue," "St. Beatrice," or "Memorial" reappear.) The name game shows up inside your congregation, too. Clever tag lines, logos, or program names in your congregation may start out as foreground identity markers, but over time they find their way into the background. One way to determine whether you're suffering from foreground envy: if you're engaged in a constant flurry of name changing, creative self-reinventions, or strategic planning within your congregation.

Big Question

What do you think drives leaders in some congregations to seek—and later discard—the latest ideas or techniques for congregational renewal?

Foreground and Background in Programs and Activities

Over time, all programs and activities move in and out of the foreground. What was once new and vital eventually becomes familiar and vital, and moves towards easily maintained or automatic. Other parts of congregational life move in the opposite direction.

Sunday schools would be a good example of both trends. For several generations Sunday schools were background functions of the congregational brain—efficiently run mechanisms of Christian formation with well-known parameters and purposes. Over the past couple of decades, however, the place and purpose of Sunday schools have been called into question, if only because many congregations find it difficult to keep Sunday schools alive and healthy. (I'd guess that you might be reading this book with "Christian formation" or "disciple making" on your attention front burner, a foreground matter above all others because it involves children.)

So in many congregations, Sunday school is no longer a background issue; it requires congregational leaders' best foreground thinking. Their unspoken goal is to create a Sunday school that eventually no longer requires foreground attention but will quietly, effectively, hum in the background.

You might think of your personal leadership in many aspects of congregational life as both background maintaining and foreground inventing. In best-case scenarios, you hope and work for programs and activities that can function smoothly without great amounts of supporting attention. Reliable leaders, effective resources and activities, and outcomes valuable to members—these characterize programs and activities that you need only to monitor from time to time. Thus assured, you can devote yourself to what's new, creative, and attention grabbing. At least that's what you hope.

> ### Trying It Out
> Make a list of ideas, people, information, or tasks that are usually in the background of your mind. Assess the reasons why each item on the list won't or can't come to the foreground of your attention. What patterns do you notice?

Frustrations with Foreground and Background

As an individual leader, you can experience major frustration when presumably background activities constantly require foreground attention. In those contexts, you prop up standing committees with your presence, you interject enthusiasm into moribund activities, you fill holes and solve problems, you repair broken trust or add hope. The frustration is that you become a maintenance worker and don't have time, energy, or will left for ideas and ideals that might contribute additional benefit to the lives of members. When this process occurs over and over, you might feel guilty of leading the congregation toward maintenance instead of mission. You want to make careful foreground and background decisions, but feel trapped in only one way of choosing.

Your congregation can experience foreground and background frustrations when the entire congregation operates continuously in a state of urgency or emergency. Making your budget (foreground) subsumes basic generosity (background). Worries about scarcity (foreground) overwhelm the quiet joy of being blessed in every way (background).

On the other hand, your congregation may disappear into the background of members' minds and thus not attract enough foreground attention to offer programs, activities, or fellowship that appeal to the community. In that case, your congregation might background itself into oblivion.

Background Isn't All Bad

You might be tempted to think that foreground is preferable to background, or that effective leaders keep most congregational matters in the foreground of members' attention. You could also reason that people who are paying attention are preferable to people who are merely monitoring their surroundings in a more or less automatic way. Or that you'll become an especially effective leader when everyone and everything is resident in some part of your foreground attention. Or that your congregation will have "arrived" when it—and, perhaps, you—are in the foreground of members' brains.

That way of thinking isn't accurate or helpful, though. It's rooted in a limited view of both your brain and your congregation. In your brain and in your congregation background is no better or worse than foreground. Your brain and your congregation necessarily shift a good share of their activities to automatic pilot. It is not possible for your brain or your congregation to constantly attend to all that they encounter. Without backgrounding mechanisms, your attention would be spread too thin over the foreground; mindfulness wouldn't be possible and you'd be scrambling to process too much information with too little brain power.

Backgrounding mechanisms are efficient primarily because certain inputs are expected and familiar—or even habitual. To ensure your congregation's overall vitality, you may first have to spend time, energy, and spirit on essential background matters such as congregational structures, relationships, and their supporting emotional tone. Then your congregation will be better able to pay attention to the foreground, which might turn out to be the growing edge of your congregation's mission and ministry.

Your Attending Brain

How do decisions about foreground and background get made? One way to frame the answers to that question is by looking at your brain's attention (and inattention) mechanisms. That's where we'll head next. In the olden days, back when information was power, scientists thought of your brain as a simple, reactive input/output mechanism, a kind of computer inside your body. Information comes in, your brain analyzes all of it, makes reasoned decisions, and goes into action. Stimulus, response. Inputs determine outcomes automatically. No emotion necessary, thank you.

In recent years, however, we have learned that this simple view of our brains just doesn't match the available evidence. Your brain's workings are much more complex than computer-based metaphors. Your neurons choose how to respond to the stimuli they encounter, including those they receive from other neurons. Your brain tags incoming stimuli with emotional markers, a process that helps you with foreground and background decisions. Perhaps least computer-like: Your brain is always anticipating, always ready for a wide range of possibilities that are embedded in constantly evolving environments, inside and outside your brain.

How does attention occur, in neurological terms? Your brain's attention sequence occurs within 1/200 of a second—or a slower 1/2 of a second in a "startle reaction," when the brain is surprised by something new. You can summarize the entire attention cycle in four verbs: arouse, orient, detect, and execute. Here's how the process of attention works.

Arousal

The brainstem—the part of your brain that connects with your spinal cord—maintains constant vigilance about its surroundings, including your body's internal state. This is the lowest level of reality monitoring, an ongoing background check. Arousal takes place when vigilance shifts to alertness, for a variety of reasons. (For example, fear is a primary arousal agent.)

Large sections of your brain—including the frontal lobes, limbic structures, and sense organs—are involved in arousal. The hippocampus—your brain's interconnected, central control center—activates long-term memory in order to find and identify the arousing agent within the vast store of your brain's mental maps.

Once aroused, your brain quickly decides whether and how to attend to the subject at hand. If your brain decides there's nothing much to pay attention to, not all of the next steps are necessary and the matter is relegated to the background. If further attention is required, all the next steps are invariably involved and the matter comes to the foreground.

Big Question

As you read about the biology of attention, think about the following questions: What does it mean to pay attention? What's the medium of exchange? Who pays? Who receives the pay? Could there be such a thing as "half price" or "two for the price of one" when it comes to attention? How do you know?

Orientation

Once aroused, your brain quickly moves to the next step. Your brain's motor centers change your body's physical orientation so that it's better able to focus its senses. Almost automatically, these changes enable the body to gather accurate information by coordinating the sensory receptors in your brain. Deep inside the thalamus, a group of neurons inhibits noise or distraction, allowing your brain to focus on the new stimulus.

An almost-universal example of orientation from congregational life is the crying baby. If a crying baby is carried out of worship during the sermon, almost every head will turn to focus on this noisome movement now become foreground. Unless the pastor does something very unusual at that moment, the crying and moving baby will attract attention away from the exquisitely chosen words of the sermon that are being delivered from behind a stationary object—the pulpit—which has now become background.

Detect

Once your body is optimally positioned, your brain decides what's normal (or safe) and what's new (or dangerous, edible, or sexually attractive). The amygdala and other parts of a novelty and reward system add rewarding emotional tags to the information, especially pleasurable sensations connected with the release of dopamine, serotonin, and endorphins. Because your brain enjoys the presence of these feel-good neurotransmitters, this may be the moment within a moment when motivation for action begins.

> **Brain Fact**
>
> Nicotine, narcotics, and alcohol inhibit your brain's natural pleasure-seeking mechanisms, setting up their own addictive mechanisms of pleasure and reward.

Execution

The entire attention sequence is completed when the frontal lobe connects all that has just occurred with long- and short-term memory. Irrelevant stimuli are blocked—by the caudate nuclei (cow-DAHT-tay NEW-clee-eye) and the basal ganglia—and motor sequences begin organizing to reach goals. In one sense, a decision has already been made.

There's Power in Attention

Before we go on to look at inattention, let's step back from brain biology for a few moments to see how background monitoring and foreground attention might connect with the concepts and practices of personal power in your congregation.

As a blessing of God for the world, your congregation is powered by the grace of God, made tangible in Word and Sacrament. As a human enterprise, your congregation is powered by grace-filled relationships. First between God and God's people, then among the people themselves.

The relationships among people in your congregation are formed and maintained because individuals attend to each other. Loving, caring, forgiving, and equipping relationships continue because the people in your congregation believe that other God-created and God-graced individuals are worthy of their attention. Because your brain is bound by the limits of time, your brain has time to pay attention to only so much information, a limited number of interactions and relationships. That means that relationships are eventually dependent on the time it takes for your brain to work well.

Relationships are framed by foreground and background choices that in turn are based on how rewarding the relationship is. When foundational elements of rewarding relationships—such as respect, regard, honor, or trust—are present over longer periods of time, those elements can be relegated to your brain's background activity. Thus your brain is afforded time to focus on the foreground elements of relationships, such as conversation, care, forgiveness, love, or concerted mutual activity.

Let me try to connect these ideas together, from the viewpoint of your personal power as a leader. You are powerful—capable of leading others in powerful actions—if your relationships are positive. Those positive relationships are created when you and another person give attention to each other. Because your brain has time for only so much activity, that foreground attention is dependent on the time-efficient backgrounding capabilities of your brain. Your personal power in your congregation is a function of your skill and wisdom in discerning how to spend your brain's time—what to pay attention to and what to assign to your brain's background activity. You are considered personally powerful when you hold others in the foreground of your brain.

Let's dress up this subject in negative clothing. You have no power if your relationships are damaged. Relationships can become damaged if your brain is constantly attending to every facet of your interactions with everyone it encounters and therefore metes out only minimal attention to each individual.

Relationships can also be damaged if you don't give any conscious attention to anyone. In that case, your brain doesn't get to choose whether to relegate interpersonal or social cues to the foreground or to the background. You could be described as having minimal social intelligence.

One other logical connector: because time is itself finite, at least as our brains experience it, time given or taken for one brain activity is not available for another. A brain that spends its time occupied with fear, anger, or anxiety may not have brain time for other emotions or brain activity.

Because attention is a function of time and because time is finite, there's not enough attention to go around. This is especially true in a too-fast world where it seems as

> **Brain Fact**
>
> Your brain can pay attention to only one thing at a time. The much-vaunted multitasking attributed to human brains is another falsely applied technological metaphor. Although computers may be able to do several things at the same time, multitasking in humans may be more accurately described as your brain's increasingly rapid shiftings of information between foreground and background. Younger and more technologically dependent individuals may appear to be multitasking when, in fact, their brains are just working quickly. At least for a few years.

though everything and everyone is scrambling for attention from everything and everyone else. So there you are, a leader relatively worthy of attention, not getting enough of what you want, need, or deserve—the attention of those you hope will follow your leadership. You have a big problem. No attention, no relationships. No relationships, no power.

Consciousness Avoided

I'd like to take a moment to exercise an author's prerogative, to tell you why I did not cover an important subject in this book. The subject

I've avoided is consciousness. You will not see its many-splendored features described here, either in reference to your brain or to your congregation.

My reasons are simple; consciousness is an enigmatic property of your brain that provides you with a sense of self—an awareness of your own existence and your relationship with the objects, people, and events you encounter. Consciousness is a subject still confusing in its complexity, still being formulated into generally accepted brain biology. When it comes to consciousness—or any of its related ideas such as awareness or self-differentiation—competing evidence, arguments, and metaphors abound.

My best guess is that the subject may never be resolved completely because of its essentially metaphoric or metaphysical nature. Because consciousness easily laps over into fields as diverse as psychology, sociology, spirituality, the nature of God, and even parapsychology, it feels like the intellectual equivalent of Silly Putty. Perhaps brain imaging technology, philosophy, and theology might someday sculpt the subject into a field of knowledge that is not as much of a mystery as it is now.

One of my favorite explanations of consciousness right now has been developed by psychiatrist and brain scholar John Ratey in his book, *The User's Guide to the Brain*. He proposes a straightforward unifying metaphor, "the brain's conductor," which he believes is located in the many intralaminar nuclei located deep inside the thalamus. The intralaminar nuclei are nerve cells with long axonal connections that project into all areas of the cerebral hemispheres and seem to coordinate the brain's oscillating "hum" at 40 hertz. If I attempted to distract you from my inadequacy as a brain science writer by making you laugh at my barely palatable puns, I'd say that Ratey's explanation sounds good to me.

Brain Fact

Laughter seems to be a function of the left hemisphere and the social brain. The strangest incident of contagious laughter occurred in 1962, when a group of schoolgirls laughed virtually nonstop for six months. The cure? Closing the schools so that these students broke off contact with each other.

The other description of a conscious brain that attracts my attention has been proposed by eminent science writer Rita Carter. She fills her newest work, *Exploring Consciousness,* with exquisite illustrations and wonderfully clear and sometimes-fanciful language, and asks readers to imagine an airplane filled with zombies. Some of these passenger-zombies control the ship's navigation, but are dependent on messages from other passenger-zombies who are sitting by windows. Each of these lower level passenger-zombies can see out only one window, which lights up in response to specific stimuli. The hapless pilots on this airship somehow make sense of the sensory mess and guide the craft to its destination, in fair and foul weather alike. Somewhere in all of the confusion, the airship could be described as conscious when a majority of the passenger-zombies sing the same song together!

Now can you see why I left consciousness out of this chapter and out of the book? Yes, the subject connects here, and yes, I'm aware of the rich possibilities embedded in the reality and imagery of the term, especially for understanding congregational identity. Perhaps my intralaminar nuclei aren't working as well as yours, or perhaps I need more windows for the passenger-zombies in my brain. Perhaps consciousness will grace the brain-and-congregations book *you* write!

Inattention Parsed

Let's get back on track now, and take some time to explore *inattention.* In strict biological terms, there is no such thing as inattention, because the brain engages all sensory stimuli in one way or another. What I'm attempting to describe here is a very real—and sometimes very problematic—characteristic of your brain when it's overloaded with stimuli and chooses to disregard inputs.

You may have thought of inattention as a lack of attention. In that way of thinking, the solution to inattention would seem simple: Attract or demand more attention. So, for example, you could recognize that sermons delivered from behind stationary objects don't allow for the brain to be attracted by movement. You would correct that inadequacy by delivering the sermon away from the pulpit and moving a lot while preaching. Completing your train of thought, you would thus conjecture that attention would be ensured and the words of the sermon rendered more capable of working their way into either the background or foreground of hearers' brains.

The matter is just a tad more complex, however. Inattention as the opposite of attention is similar to the false idea that sleep is the opposite of wakefulness, that sleep is when your brain shuts down for awhile.

What is inattention, then? It's a naturally occurring and necessary function of your brain's attention sequence. Even when it seems inattentive, your brain is still attending to the stimuli it perceives. Under some conditions, and for the sake of the body mechanisms that protect and nurture it, your brain purposefully sloughs off—into long-term memory, perhaps—some of what its sense organs encounter. Through inattention, your brain improves useful attention by actively shutting off awareness of sensory inputs that do not match or contribute to what your brain's control center has decided is attention-worthy. Then, absent the noise of competing sensory input, your brain quickly and efficiently focuses on the matter it cares about and completes the attention sequence without distraction.

Brain Fact

What's the function of sleep for the brain? Several possibilities are being tested. The two kinds of sleep—rapid eye movement (REM) and non-REM (quiet) sleep—might (1) enable brain cells to repair themselves; (2) help some neurotransmitters regain full sensitivity; (3) allow brain development in babies and infants; and (4) prepare the brain's coping mechanisms for danger upon waking. During REM sleep, the amygdala communicates with the anterior cingulate gyrus (an-TEER-ee-or SING-you-layt JYE-ruhs) and the occipital lobes, perhaps attaching emotions to dreams and memories.

How are inattention and background related? In the metaphors that plague my mind, inattention feels like background monitoring with a dash of self-protecting disregard thrown in. Because backgrounded stimuli are still important for the brain's work, inattention allocates the stimuli to a place further down the attentional ladder, deeper into the parts of the brain where little light shines.

Another useful metaphor here: Your brain is always attending to the "garage band" of its internal and external surroundings, but it doesn't stick a microphone next to everything or everyone in the band. Your brain needs to distinguish the difference between music and noise, when to play along with the band and when to walk away. That's why inattention mechanisms are, in some ways, more complex than the elements of attention. Purposeful inattention occurs throughout your brain, in specifically named brain areas or organs. Like backgrounding, inattention is also a generic function of the entire brain. Many brain structures process information by limiting it, maintaining a delicate tension between receiving and inhibiting information. The hypothalamus, the brain's control center, is a good example of this dual-functioning brain structure.

Glial cells also help you manage attention. They may comprise another brain system that is only now becoming known. There are several types of glial cells, located in every nook and cranny of your brain. The quantity of glial cells is nine or ten times greater than the number of neurons. One function of glial cells is to limit or direct the strength and frequency of neuronal activity. Two types of glial cells seem to be involved in inhibiting attention:

- One kind controls the metabolism of neurons and their function. The slower the metabolism, the slower the cells fire.
- Another type coats the axons of neurons with myelin (MY-eh-linn), a fatty substance that controls the rate at which axons process information. Some researchers have likened myelin to the insulation on wires. Less well-insulated cell axons are not as efficient in transmitting neuronal impulses to other neurons.

Another attention-managing brain structure is the amygdala (ah-MIHG-duh-lah). (Actually, there are two of these almond-shaped structures in the front middle part of your brain, but they are commonly referred to in the singular.) About a dozen tiny nodules comprise this tiny brain structure. Each nodule is connected to many brain regions and interacts with a complex set of hormones and neurotransmitters. Together with your brain's pleasure center the amygdala determines whether information is beneficial and/or actionable. For example, the amygdala is heavily involved in your brain's ability to recognize faces (and the emotions they display), which enables group cooperation and the resolution of social ambiguity.

Foreground and Background
Choices Made Difficult

It's tough for your brain to make foreground and background choices when it's overburdened with information. For more than a few years and in almost every facet of human society, the variety and quantity of information you encounter has increased. The quantity of data has increased, certainly, but so have the accessibility and the speed of data. Even the rates of increase themselves have increased. This is true especially in the Western world, where we think of information primarily in terms of its technological sources or processors. Most likely, more and more of your time is spent in dealing with information you may or may not seek, but which nevertheless crowds your time and your brain's capacities.

Brain Fact

Some brain scientists think that depression is strongly connected to inattention. When depressed, your brain uses only a minimal amount of brain chemicals—serotonin, for example—and is therefore less capable of any kind of action. The technical term for this depression-laden inactivity is *psychomotor retardation.*

Data reach you at every place in your daily life, whether by your invitation or not. Your cars; appliances; pew racks; home entertainment systems; clothing; sanctuary walls, doors, and windows; and playthings—all throw information at you. You are beset and besotted with information overload in your kinships, friendships, and memberships. Newsletters, broadcast e-advocacy alerts, temple talks, program commercials projected on screens before worship services, targeted mailings, outlined teaching sermons, program brochures, telephone trees, inserts in worship materials, contribution envelopes, "disastergrams" about recent calamities, word-heavy Web sites—each piles on top of the other, hoping to attract your limited foreground attention. Background and foreground choices become difficult because there are too many decisions to make in too little time.

When you encounter too much information, your brain may be harmed by that encounter. In the next chapter we'll talk about fear and stress, but here's a teaser: Under severe stress—which can include overwhelming amounts of information—your brain's hip-pocampus can be harmed so that it can't quite consolidate explicit memories of an event for later use.

Brain Fact

Those too-frequent moments of sudden forgetfulness? They're called "overload aphasia" and may be evidence of the harm that comes to brains trying to process too much information too quickly. These moments are not restricted to seniors.

The Cycle of Inattention

You could think of inattention as your brain's response to information overload. Inattention increases among individuals and groups of people in a fairly predictable pattern. Let me illustrate this self-perpetuating process as it might play out when you try to provide what you consider to be useful information to those you lead. The cycle of inattention consists of several parts, each causing or giving sustenance to the next part.

- The cycle begins with your strong desire to teach, persuade, influence, change, or otherwise affect individuals regarding a particular subject or possible action. You have the best intentions in mind.
- Because you're competing for people's attention, you send large amounts of what you perceive to be high-quality information (sensory input) to the brains of your desired audience.
- Because they are already overburdened with information, others' brains select and attend only to a small portion of your information, perhaps only cognitively at best.
- Actively or passively, the information-receivers send back to you the

unfortunate news that they aren't accepting a good share of what you're sending. Some of your information has been transferred to their brains' background, but most has been ignored.

- The cycle now repeats itself more intensely. You redouble your efforts to move information into the brains of your intended audience, perhaps thinking that you'll be more clever or more insistent this time around. You speak more loudly, send messages more frequently, and use more interactive media.

- Predictably, the brains of the information-receivers work even harder to set aside what they didn't ask for: more information. Stress increases, emotional neutrality sets in, and fight, flight, and freeze mechanisms start to kick in. (See the next chapter.) You wonder whether to repeat the cycle even more cleverly than before or to give up entirely on the notion that anyone would pay attention to you about anything.

- You decide to read the book, *Your Brain Goes to Church*. (Okay, okay, I made up the last step in the cycle, but you get the picture, yes?)

As a purveyor of information, you get to choose how and when to send particular information. The brains of information-receivers, however, behave more or less automatically as they protect themselves from information overload and from those who create that problem. The harder you push information at others' brains, the more you risk the reciprocating inattention of the very individuals you seek to influence. Or, the more you insist on being in the foreground, the more likely you'll be pushed to the background, or even out the brain's back door.

Faster and Faster Isn't Good, Either

You may try to solve the too-much-information problem simply by working faster. That solution may seem effective, but only temporarily and partially so. According to recent theory, one part of your brain—the cognitive system—may gradually learn to process more and more information faster and faster. But other brain functions—notably the emotional system—may not have that capability, running at a more-or-less fixed speed no matter how much information comes in. The result may very well be that your slower-running emotional system cannot reliably mark all the information that the faster-running cognitive system processes.

The effects of that function-slippage may be ominous. You may make fewer decisions using emotional and altruistic thought. Emotional neutrality may be another way of describing how your information-overloaded brain just can't attach emotional value to most inputs, and so processes information only cognitively. One possible result of this whole chain of cause-and-effect: your brain may become emotionally inert, and increasingly yield ethically impaired or morally rudderless decisions. To say it another way, your emotional intelligence might diminish considerably.

Attention and Inattention in Your Congregation

Attention and inattention are important to your role as a congregational leader, and may show up in your leader-brain in the following places:

- Do you fret about irrelevance or wonder why no one reads your parish newsletter?
- Do you sigh sadly because your spiffy congregational Web site gathers electronic dust and spider webs?
- When you look around at other congregations and their leaders, does it seem that what's lurid and loud gets paid attention to, while the messages of quiet and calm leaders get ignored?
- Do you think of yourself as the victim of a congregation-wide attention deficit disorder?

It's understandable that you might feel that way about your leadership in your congregation, because the same kinds of questions are being asked everywhere in society. It is an overriding truth about these times that most of us aren't paying attention to most things most of the time because too many of us are chasing too few attentive brains with too much information. Because attention is limited in quantity and availability, it's the prime commodity of our hassled and harried lives. Not enough of us are staying in one place long enough to take in information and reflect on it. Too much information is just data waiting to be recognized, by attentive brains, as knowledge—and too much knowledge crowds out wisdom.

That's the attentional environment in which you—and the members of your congregation—live and work. At the same time, it's the context into which God has placed you, for good and godly reasons.

Big Question

What makes you think that your brand of information, your message, or your favorite cause is somehow exempt from information overload? How do you take into account other people's brains' capacity for not paying attention to you?

Stepping Away from Inattention

How might you correct this continuing condition, at least in the life of the church? Well, there's always praying for Judgment Day to come soon, personally contributing to the collapse of Western civilization as you know it and, of course, hoping that the Chicago Cubs will win the World Series (thus causing the resulting catastrophe in hell).

But there's another, simpler way for you to solve this inattention problem in your congregation. Focus on the members. A simple maxim might express one solution to the attention deficit that burdens you: "In order to gain attention, give it first." In other words, fill your brain's foreground and background with the people you love and serve.

Why does "attend to others first" work? Because social reciprocity seems to be hardwired in our brains, it's reasonable to expect that the people to whom you give careful attention will feel a deep obligation to reciprocate with similar behaviors and attitudes towards you and, by extension, your congregation.

Getting to Specifics

Following are some specific behaviors that you might engage in, each of which carries the subtle message, "My dear friend, your well-being occupies the foreground and background of my mind." Try any of these actions, by yourself or together with other leaders in your congregation.

- In all publicity, invitations, and communications, state the specific benefits that will come to those who participate, so that they can better serve God and witness to Christ.

- Practice the techniques and attitudes of presence, literally and figuratively. Purge from your behaviors the subtle clues that you're only partially present, or have something more important to do and someone more important to pay attention to. For example, the behavior I most need to get rid of is continuing to work at a task while conversing with someone.

> **Brain Fact**
>
> The brain's "readiness potential" is a way of describing how the brain unconsciously prepares for an action about ½ a second before the decision for action is made. The actual muscle contraction takes place another ½ second later. In a sense, your brain knows before you know it and is always "ready."

- Change the content of your conversations so that in all your encounters with others you learn about their lives of faithful service in the world. Start with strangers, service personnel, quiet people, or others you might have overlooked in the past.
- Use asset-based or appreciative inquiry methods to plan and conceptualize your congregation's mission.
- Where possible, personalize your communications and interactions with others. Try a quiet approach.
- Insist on relationship-building goals as part of everything you do as a leader.

- Identify the places, processes, and people in your "information pipelines" where attention is getting stuck or sloughed off. Reestablish your relationships with leaders who are already attentive partners in your work.
- Use private and public devotional moments to pray for specific people inside and outside the inner circle of loyal congregational leaders.
- Start building a culture of gratitude within your congregation. Select a number of individuals who will join you for several months in an informal effort to spread gratitude throughout your congregation. It all starts with speaking a heartfelt word of thanks and looking your benefactor square in the eyes.
- If you have a congregational database, include fields for items such as "hobbies," "family," "vocation," or "special notes."
- Attend congregational events in their entirety, participating in activities so that a rich fabric of friendships can be built in conversation and shared activities. Don't overlook informal opportunities, such as late-night watering holes and community events in which members participate.
- From time to time, map all the categories of people whom you know well enough to call "friend." Marvel at the size and scope of relationships with which you have been blessed. Keep your map in plain view for awhile.
- Before and after worship services, keep to a minimum your conversations with "important people," and increase your availability to those who might otherwise be ignored.
- Set aside one hour a week to reconnect with individuals who you want to keep track of, learn more about, learn from, or assist. Use e-mail or the telephone.

A Hopeful Note

Whenever you are tempted to think of yourself as someone assigned to permanent background status in the minds of others, remember that you have the personal power to correct that feeling by offering your loving regard to the people you serve. Remember that, because of Christ's redemptive life, death, and resurrection, God's attentive love is always focused on your ministry. Count on God's presence in your life. In God's mind, you're always foreground material. God speaks your language, for heaven's sake!

Big Question(s)

Answer any of these questions about the style or content of the language you use to assure others that you are paying attention to them:

- How do your publicity, registration, and news-sharing communications rate on readability formulas?
- Whose jargon is the default vocabulary in your congregation? For example, how frequently are the "alphabet soups" of the church standard fare in communication or publicity pieces?
- What's the tone or direction of your conversations about others? Where is it positive, affirming, or appreciative? Where does it approach whining, carping, or gossiping?
- How aware are you about contemporary trends in communication styles, emerging idiomatic expressions, or preferred means of communication?

Looking Ahead

In chapter 4 we'll continue the conversation, this time focusing on another fascinating and important piece of neuroscience: danger and opportunity. You'll see how fear shows up in your congregation's life. Get ready for the chapter by looking inside yourself—as a congregational leader—and asking yourself, "What, really, am I afraid of?"

Exploring Further

Find a small group of people you'd like to do some "plain talking" with. Use any of the following questions or suggested activities to get started.

1. Where did you think the idea "No hablo español" was heading when you started reading the chapter? How does the direction you imagined connect with the subjects that eventually unfolded?

2. Where did the chapter's conversation stop short of what you expected? How would you have continued?

3. Find a trusted friend and talk about one or more of the "zingers" that got under your skin just a little bit. What happened inside you, and why did it happen?

4. Write a responsive prayer or confession that specifies the ways in which you (and others) really don't pay all that much attention to each other. Talk about a time and place to actually use what you've written.

5. What's more important to think and talk about: attention or inattention? Why?

6. The chapter left out all kinds of material about attention; for example, attention-deficit disorders and improper ways to get attention. Talk about what's missing, and how those subjects affect the life of your congregation.

7. How do you decide who or what stays in the foreground attention of your brain, and who or what slips into background maintenance?

Chapter 4

You Can't Avoid
What Won't Go Away

Danger and Opportunity

SOME THINGS JUST WON'T GO AWAY, even if you want them to. Syrupy greeting cards endure, a toddler with a fetid diaper insists on being noticed, or stray kittens wrap themselves around your ankle.

The subjects of this chapter are another example of things that won't go away. I know, because I tried to avoid two of them while tap-tapping the first drafts of this chapter into my computer. In its earlier versions, this chapter was only about fear, a long-standing favorite subject of mine. Because fear grows like dandelions in the minds of most church leaders, I thought it would be a slam-dunk subject for a book on brain science and congregations. Fear would be sufficient.

One problem is that danger and opportunity wouldn't let go of me. The village of people who have contributed to this book's shape and direction, and who I acknowledged earlier, were fairly unanimous: "Fear isn't as important as what lies under it, behind it, before it, over it, throughout it." (In this village, prepositions are a big thing.) Danger and opportunity kept tugging at my shirtsleeves, kept edging into my fingers, kept needling me. So I have chosen to yield to the inevitable truth that you can't avoid what won't go away, especially when it involves danger and opportunity.

In this chapter, we're going to look at both danger and opportunity, at the emotions that accompany them (especially fear), and at the ways you can choose between them. It'll be my job to help you pay attention to what won't go away, and your job to read the whole chapter!

Big Picture: Danger and Opportunity

Every stimulus you encounter every day is brimming with the possibility of either danger or opportunity. You live within multiple environments that are both harmful and helpful. To survive or even prosper, you make conscious and unconscious choices about the inputs your senses take in. Seize the opportunity or dispatch with the danger. Sometimes the choices are difficult. (More on that thought later in the chapter.)

Brain Fact

Oxytocin, a peptide produced by the brain's limbic structures, is the new chemical to watch for in coming decades. Oxytocin is a major factor in most affiliative behavior, including parent-child bonding, love and lovemaking, social intelligence, and lifelong bonding. (And you thought serotonin was the neurotransmitter to watch!)

Everyday examples abound. You decide what foods to eat, based on your perception of their potential for harm or good. You size up strangers—by the look of their faces, most likely—within mere seconds of meeting them. You make conscious danger-or-opportunity choices about the speed with which you will drive your automobile, the clothes you will wear, the sermons you'll preach or listen to, the words you'll use in conversation, and the products you will purchase. Each choice presents the possibility for danger or opportunity, or sometimes both.

Automatic brain/body functions offer potential danger and opportunity as well. Take breathing as an example. Every breath you take could present both danger (chemical pollution, viral and bacterial contaminants, or pollen) and opportunity (oxygen, pleasing aromas, the chance to expel carbon dioxide). Although the choice is rarely conscious, your body-connected brain chooses between danger and opportunity every time you take a breath. If you suffer from respiratory disease or have difficulty breathing, the choices are made in the foreground of your brain's attention system.

Whether conscious (foreground) or unconscious (background), your danger and opportunity choices are intended to yield your survival. Your brain wants its home—your body—to stay alive. So you choose, at every moment, what will enhance your chances to live past that moment. Your brain also wants to be alive among other people—you're a social being—and so you assess danger and opportunity as you encounter other people. Your family, your colleagues, your congregation—each group is bound to you. In some cases, others participate in the danger and opportunity choices and share with you the effects of those choices.

There's nothing wrong with that kind of choosing, and there's nothing selfish about it, either. In fact, if you were a stewardship-savvy person, you'd say that this survival thing only makes sense, given God's abundant investment in the enterprise with "you" as the brand name. God expects a good return (see various parables of Jesus) and so wants you to stay alive and out of danger. God also has a lot of work to get done, and you're a major player in God's mission to the world.

Facing danger and opportunity is not just an individual matter. *You* is also a plural pronoun, and throughout this book *you* includes the con-

---

Big Question ?

You thought God made use only of the most sterling of your qualities? Remember the story of Balaam's donkey in Numbers 22? The God who could make a donkey into an instrument of prophecy certainly can make use of your fearfulness as well as your courage. You can count on it!

---

gregation in which you are a leader. Your congregation has been formed—by water and the Spirit—to be a purpose-fulfilling enterprise in God's scheme of things. As a brain comprised of individual brains, your congregation wants its body—the formal institution—to stay alive, and so makes choices about what might be danger and what might be an opportunity.

Your brain can respond in a variety of ways when it meets up with danger and opportunity. Fear is your brain's immediate response to danger. Responses to opportunity include reasoned acceptance of possibilities as well as seemingly unreasonable risk-taking. When you are faced with clear choices about danger or opportunity, you make them quickly, based on hardwired or memory-laden learned responses. When the choices are ambiguous or unfamiliar, you take a little more time, rolling various scenarios or possibilities through your frontal cortex before coming to a decision.

A challenge for your decision-making brain—your individual brain as well as for the collected brains in your congregation—is that what might be dangerous at one moment or for one brain could turn out to be an opportunity at another moment or for another brain. For example, a speeding car is dangerous if it's coming toward you on your side of the road but it might offer great joy if you are soaring down an open highway toward a pleasurable destination. Or, one congregational leader might see your congregation's financial difficulty as perilous while another leader might view the situation as an opportunity to chew over basic questions about your congregation's purpose.

Brain Fact

In stressful situations, the hypothalmus (high-poh-THAL-muss) starts a chain reaction of immediate reaction. The brain releases floods of chemicals: CRF, the brain's own stress hormone (which signals other hormone releases); cortisol and adrenaline (which prepare you for action); pituitary hormones (which signal every major gland of the body to secrete their hormones).

So, danger and opportunity decisions face you in every part of your life. First, you choose which is which, then how to react. The choices are sometimes simple and automatic; at other times they are complex and difficult to make.

Next, let's take apart "danger and opportunity" from the perspective of your brain and your congregation. Then we'll spend time examining fear from the same vantage points.

You Can't Avoid What Won't Go Away

Let's start with danger. Your brain keeps choosing to identify situations as dangerous. That's the most effective way that your body protects your brain, ensuring its well-being and survival. You have inherited over the millennia the automatic capacity to choose as dangerous just about anything and everything in your environment, including other people. By reacting to danger with fear, you avoid or defend against real or imagined dangers, diminishing their presence and their effect. This assures a longer life span and higher quality life for yourself. At least that's how it's supposed to work.

Opportunity won't go away because your brain responds favorably to stimuli that increase its pleasure. Your brain also displays an innate capacity to create or find novelty. Your brain wants to enhance the physical and social environment in which your body lives. Your brain wants to do more than just avoid perceived danger in always fearful responses. (More later on this subject.)

Emotions won't go away, either. Although you may not be aware of them, your primary emotions are the foundations for the decisions you make between danger and opportunity. Once your brain's arousal system has identified variations from what's normal, the amygdala attaches identifying emotional tags (biological barcodes?) to that information and informs the rest of your brain about the results of the tagging. Some of the tags—various combinations of neurotransmitters flooding synapses—are positive and have names such as surprise and happiness. Others are negative and have names such as fear, anger, and disgust. Emotions are the key to the analysis that soon follows. Your forebrain integrates the information with available memories of similar stimuli. Emotions help your brain determine whether you are competent to face the challenge implicit in the information you have encountered. If the analysis is basically optimistic, you approach the challenge joyfully, and secondary emotions such as trust and anticipation are engaged. If the analysis is basically pessimistic, a state of sadness invokes other emotions, such as grief or more fear and anger. (Later in this chapter I'll suggest another possible way for your brain to analyze information—a pragmatic approach.)

Primary and secondary emotions give rise to feelings—emotions that you recognize at a conscious level. When the feelings persist over a period of time, they're called moods. Large patterns of feelings are called temperaments. (There are two basic temperaments: bold or uninhibited and anxious or inhibited.) Your temperaments develop by age two and can last a lifetime.

Danger Is Real

Some elements of life are universally recognized as dangerous. The forces of the natural world can create life-ending events such as tornadoes, lava flows, fires, or floods. People and creatures that might want to consume or kill you are always dangerous. A handful of airline peanuts in your mouth might be toxic if you are allergic to nuts. Lack of food and water, unsafe housing, the oppressive greed of powerful others—these are always dangerous.

Potential danger is also real, if only because your brain chooses to call it so. The power of the potential danger to influence your action depends on how well your brain can recall and reassemble long- and short-term memories of similar circumstances. You might think of a phone call from a marketing firm as dangerous if you have experienced identity theft. A new pastor might be dangerous to your well-being if you disagree with his or her theology.

When you're dealing with danger, "now" is the only moment that matters, and so you make quick decisions with little or no thought (literally!) about the full range of consequences that might follow those decisions. Your only (non)thought: how to dispatch with the danger.

The Reality of Opportunities

As far as your brain is concerned, opportunities are as real as danger. When a stimulus is perceived as an opportunity, your brain marshals its resources to take advantage of the situation. Feel-good chemicals (described in previous chapters) flood neural receptors. Absent the nearly paralyzing effects of fear, your brain is better able to integrate rational and emotional responses to stimuli, and to call forth motor responses in a variety greater than its limited fight, flee, or freeze responses to fear. More of your brain is available to more of your brain!

When your brain decides that information presents an opportunity, it alows time for other or better decisions. "Now" isn't the only time on your brain's clock. So when conversation in the church council grows tense, you don't let your brain's fear reactions immediately take charge and mislabel your detractors as enemies. You take the time to choose helpful body language and words. Your brain's sensory structures use the extra time to check more carefully the full range of the input they have received, for its accuracy and utility.

Opportunity-choices make planning possible because logical or sequential thought enters the picture. Your brain weighs the varied outcomes of imagined or remembered scenarios, as well as their relative

---

Trying It Out

With someone you trust, contrast your memories of times you were afraid with times when you seized an opportunity. Think together about your state of mind at those moments, what you were willing to do, how you felt about the people around you, your spiritual state of mind. If possible, make a chart of your answers.

---

advantages. Imagination and curiosity—powerful engines for creativity and motivation—have a chance to flourish. Instead of verbally smashing your supposed-enemies into bloodless pulp, you can imagine—or even empathize with—their feelings or thoughts.

When your brain chooses to frame information as opportunity, your social brain—structures and functions that allow you to relate to others—counteracts the individualistic choices of fear responses. Opportunity-choices allow for pleasurable and life-enhancing interactions with other brains. Opportunities draw you together with other people, in common purpose and for mutual benefit.

In summary, when your brain chooses to regard a situation as an opportunity instead of as a danger, the "Urgent for Survival" sign gets taken down and is replaced by a different one: "Important for Longer-term Well-being."

The Biology of Opportunity: Your Social Brain

"Your social brain" is a metaphor for the ways your brain helps you live with other humans with empathy and love. Your social brain goes to church as you—together with others—choose to seize opportunities.

The social brain is not found in a single location in your brain. Instead, it consists of many parts scattered around your brain. Here are some of your social brain's structures and functions:

- The amygdala helps sort out social ambiguity.
- The cerebellum coordinates the relationships among emotions, memories, language, and actions.
- Various frontal lobe regions of the cortex process feelings and pain that can bias decision-making, analyze social information from other brain regions, and detect errors and incongruity in social interaction.
- The right hemisphere of your cortex analyzes nonverbal communication; its parietal lobe helps you relate to yourself and others in physical space.
- The left hemisphere of your cortex processes language—essential in social interaction.

When they operate in concert, the structures in the social brain allow you to love, feel, and show empathy, judge emotion and intent in others, experience shame, guilt, and forgiveness. The social brain helps you inhibit aggression, increase your social bonding, integrate your moral decisions with actions, learn social skills, and maintain an overall sense of your self.

A social brain that is working well transcends both selfish and self-loathing behaviors in order to benefit self and others. Another, familiar description for those who follow Christ: a social brain "has the mind of Christ" (Phil. 2:5-11).

Big Question

How much of religious education might be a matter of developing the social brain within a theological setting?

The Reality of Fear

Fear isn't always bad. In its most helpful manifestations, fear enables you to avoid quickly what's immediately harmful. From a theological viewpoint, fear places your life in context—as a dependent creature of an awe-inspiring and loving God—and makes human community necessary. Fear is an early warning system that helps you instantaneously balance risk with safety. Without any fear, you might be called fearless, but would most likely not survive long. Fear is so necessary for your survival that you have been endowed with three interconnected fear systems:

- A primitive fear system, that operates in the first one-tenth of a second after an initial stimulus, not dependent on either conscious or rational processes.
- A rational fear system that kicks in a few thousandths of a second later, after having analyzed the sensory data.
- Consciousness itself—the potential actions of the entire brain—that mediate what the first two systems have discovered.

What else to know about fear? When it gets to be a habit and finds enough words, fear is called anxiety. If anxieties become habituated over time, they're called phobias and heighten self-destructive behaviors in individuals and groups. Fear systems are both generic—not dependent on a single stimulus to be activated—and specific. So, for example, an airline pilot could be terrified of being inside tall buildings but be unafraid of flying a high-soaring airplane. A generic fear of heights would not describe this person's fear.

Fear of real and perceived danger is everywhere. Fear sells newspapers, soap, body-enhancing products, relationship-building drugs, presidential candidates, and religious agendas. Fear is easily taught and easily learned, even in the church. You can learn to fear danger in Sunday school, sermons, Christian radio, Christian parenting classes, half-truthed harangues, and wild-eyed Web sites. Fear is the dominant emotion among nation states. Terror has become an effective tool for political rhetoric. Fear-inspiring leaders prosper, if only among their followers. Around the world, millions of professional workers—soldiers, journalists, legislators, law-enforcement officers, clergy, philosophers, insurance agents—spend their lives dissecting, describing, diffusing, or defeating fear.

Fear is efficient—almost any stimulus can cause your brain to choose danger and your brain to respond with fear. Fear requires little maintenance in order to remain effectual. Because it's contagious in groups, especially groups crowded together physically or emotionally, fear spreads quickly. Once it splashes into human communities, fear is difficult to dissipate as it ripples back and forth across the ponds of life.

The Biology of Fear

Among all human characteristics, full-blown fear involves the whole body, as illustrated by the following laundry list of organs and brain structures involved in primal fear:

- Thanks to the thalamus, the amygdala perceives the general shape of a fearful object or situation. The amygdala sounds the general alarm.
- The amygdala marks the threat and stores it in memory, most likely in the hypothalamus, the brain's vaunted control center.
- Signaled by the pituitary gland—"the master gland" of the body—adrenaline floods the body.
- The thyroid gland raises the body's metabolic rate.
- The liver breaks down glycogen so that energy is instantly available for the higher metabolic rate.
- Normal but marginally necessary body systems shut down, digestion stops, saliva dries up, and skin temperature drops.
- Blood is redirected to muscles for fleeing, fighting, or freezing.
- Pupils dilate, ready to send danger signals to the visual thalamus.
- The lung's bronchioles dilate in order to make oxygen usage more efficient.
- Breathing quickens to take in more oxygen.
- Body hairs bristle, perhaps to cool the skin, activate muscles in the limbs, or heighten overall alertness.
- The bladder and colon prepare to empty themselves in preparation for possible violence or injury.
- The spleen contracts, adding more white blood cells and platelets to the blood supply.
- Heart and blood pressure rates increase, so that the brain and body have available optimum amounts of oxygen.

All of these responses happen within mere seconds unless the "general alarm" is called off by the brain's second and third systems, the rational and conscious responses to fearsome stimuli.

Trying It Out

The next time you're fearful, or you're in a group that seems to be characterized by fear, take a quick inventory of which of the physical manifestations of fear are evident. Granted, you're not going to be able to measure the hormonal output of your adrenal medulla, but you can probably sense the temperature or clamminess of your skin, for example. Think about this question: What might happen in your work as a congregational leader if you were able more quickly to spot those physical symptoms in yourself or in others?

Fear can become habitual, as your brain builds neuronal pathways to make its responses even more efficient. Once your thalamus and amygdala—coconspirators in the primal fear sequence—get used to a specific fear stimulus, they need even less time to search your brain's memory to match a general pattern of sensory input to the now-familiar danger. Your heightened body systems kick into gear even more quickly and readily, and the neuronal pathway gradually turns into an eight-lane neuronal freeway with only a few off-ramps.

Whether habituated to fear or not, your brain does not naturally intend fear responses to last past the short moments when the brain compels your body to react

Brain Fact

The direct effect of repeated neuronal stimulation is called long-term potentiation (LTP). In LTP, communication among oft-used synapses is strengthened, increasing the potential over time that the same set of synapses will fire. LTP in the amygdala (a primary locus of fear responses) and in the hippocampus (one location for long-term memory) could explain why fear is so easily turned into anxiety and stress.

to perceived danger. Once the danger has passed, your brain is flooded with endorphins, one of your brain's feel-good chemicals, and the pleasure of escape replaces the terror of possible danger. The fear sequence is complete.

To maintain its body in a continuing state of preparedness for fighting, fleeing, or freezing, your brain puts itself and your body at risk. Over the long term, few of the physiological changes inherent in fear bode well for your body's overall health. (Think, for example, about the effects of continuing higher blood pressure or heartbeat rates.) Fear-based behaviors, short- or long-term, suppress the immune system. Higher levels of fear-induced hormones can inhibit functioning memory in your brain. The rapid expenditure of energy in fear responses deprives the rest of your body of needed nutrients. Because your brain seeks pleasure and long-term survival, it does not want to maintain a constant state of fearfulness, stress, or anger. Continuing fear forces your brain to rewire itself into an eventually destructive pattern of reactive behavior.

A Note about Stress

The general description and physical components of stress are similar to those of fear. Neurologically, both eustress (good stress, such as happiness) and distress (bad stress, such as worry) involve similar sequences of brain activity, and result in similar physiological consequences. Although early brain literature rarely named fear as a close biological correlative to stress, current research and writing sometimes combine the two into a larger family of human emotion.

Recently revised research reveals an important fact: the supposedly typical fight, flight, and freeze reactions to primal stress or fear are actually more typical of males. Female reactions to stress more closely approximate "tend and befriend," an increase in nurturing behaviors. Male responses directly benefit the individual facing stressful situations; female responses also benefit the group. The difference between male and female responses can be attributed to the relative strength of predominate neurotransmitters: testosterone and vasopressin in males, and estrogen and oxytocin in women.

A Note about Anger

The biology of another universally human emotion, anger, seems to be connected to the mechanisms of fear. Confronted with danger, the human brain typically chooses from among three basic responses: fighting, fleeing, or freezing. If you choose fighting as the primary response, it makes sense to your brain next to call up anger because anger takes advantage of your body's capacity for aggression.

The normal human brain does not readily choose fighting and anger, because aggressive behavior can turn out to be more hazardous to your well-being than the simple responses of motionless freezing or rapid flight. Habituated or constantly recurring anger has the same harmful physical effects as constantly recurring fear. Unchecked, continuing patterns of aggression also result in diminished social bonds that help maintain human community. How does that happen? The frontal lobes of aggressive individuals are often underdeveloped. Lacking the brain power to sustain focus and block irrelevant stimuli, these individuals find it difficult to restrain impulses or apply wisdom in a given situation.

The apostle Paul offers this advice for a healthy brain: "Don't get so angry that you sin. Don't go to bed angry and don't give the devil a chance" (Eph. 4:26 CEV).

Danger and Fear Go to Church

In congregations and the wider church, danger and fear can operate in the resources, programs, relationships, or structures of these spiritual enterprises. Church leaders like you are regularly tempted—sometimes by church leaders like me—to see dangers all around, to react fearfully, and to allay your fears with our latest sure-fire solutions to your fearsome difficulty. In a fearful environment, spiritual enemies are easily imagined (or constructed) and righteous fervor is easily colored with the scarlet hues of fear.

Trying It Out

Find several items that claim to be spiritually enlightening, such as newsletters, Web sites, journals, or mass mailings. Read each item with a "Finding Danger" filter and see how the writers or editors might be using fear as a tool for their purposes. Think about what you might say or do to counteract those tones or emphases.

You may not regard your congregation as a place of danger—you may not see any toothsome predators roaming your sanctuary, seeking "whom they may devour." Still, devilish fear may be more prevalent in your congregation than you realize, whether in the brains of individual members or in your congregational brain.

Fear might naturally occur at moments when distress or disaster threaten you and other leaders, either imminently or on your distant-but-imagined horizons. Danger and fear might show up in your congregation during conflict. It might hide inside diminished trust, lack of empathy, increased pettiness, decreased generosity, or broken communication links. Small fears may show up when you elect leaders, count weekly offerings, read denominational publications, prepare a sermon, or facilitate a meeting.

Brain Fact

In the past, schizophrenia was attributed to problems with dopamine signaling in particular brain systems, such as the basal ganglia, the frontal lobe, the hippocampus, the limbic system, and the auditory system. Now brain scientists are looking at impaired signaling from a different brain chemical, glutamate, as a more likely cause for this disease. Schizophrenia affects about 2,000,000 people in the United States annually. About 60 percent of people with this disorder have a high likelihood of becoming substance abusers. A disproportionately large share of people with schizophrenia are chronically homeless.

If you think about the future as essentially danger-filled, fear might inhibit your planning processes, most of which implicitly depend on hope, courage, vision, or other nonfearful emotions. If you're a fearful leader—constantly identifying most situations as dangerous—you might experience great difficulty guiding others through successful processes for visioning, writing mission statements, or summarizing your congregation's core values.

Danger-choices might invade decision-making when supposedly democratic processes—the majority "wins"—push aside group consensus or entrepreneurial leadership. When your first reactions to new ideas or possibilities are always negative, your reactions might reflect that danger-choices have already taken over your spirit. Fear is most likely a defining characteristic of your congregation if "naming, blaming, and shaming" behaviors predominate in meetings, personal conversations, and congregational relationships. Fear is most likely the underlying reason why distant "they's" are excoriated for their supposedly authoritarian, arrogant, neglectful, inept, or otherwise danger-causing behaviors. Several kinds of imagined danger are probably at the heart of your worry about asking congregation members for financial contributions. Your brain may engage in an interior argument as you try to decide which is the greater danger: asking people for money, or not having enough money to maintain your congregation's vital ministries.

Why lay these and other negative congregational characteristics at the doorstep of danger and the fear that usually follows? Because fearful reactions to danger—fighting, fleeing and freezing—are present in almost all negative or destructive congregational behaviors.

Even though the good news of God in Christ Jesus is fear-reducing and although love does diminish fear, it's a sad fact that many members of the body of Christ are overly aware of danger and fearful.

What Makes Fear Go Away?

The subhead above is a little misleading, because the capacity of the human brain to be fearful never goes away. Every newborn hardwired brain comes with "fear-responsive" as part of its basic equipment. Still, fear can be diminished, its effects ameliorated, its sequences overridden.

Fear is *not* quickly reduced by rational considerations. Why? At the height of fearfulness—and remember that anger and stress are in the same family of emotional reactions—the rational or sequential functions of your brain literally are short-circuited by the amygdala and the rest of the quick-response fear mechanisms. You aren't capable of rational thought, at least for awhile.

Most fear-reducing mechanisms of your brain depend on your relationships with others. In the language of Christian theology, you reduce your fears because you are part of God's community. The church not only mediates God's grace—in Word and Sacrament—but also makes that grace real for you in daily repentance and forgiveness. As a graced and forgiven servant of God you support and protect others, offering

Bonus Reading: Fear Not and Fear God

You properly fear your completely transcendent and powerful God, but because of Christ Jesus you also know that God loves you. You don't have to be a prisoner of your biological predisposition to be a fearful creature of habit. You can fear God and experience the freedom of Christ's redemption because of what God reveals in the Scriptures.

The Bible has much to say about fear. In its 25 Hebraic forms, the word *fear* occurs over 750 times in the Scriptures; 10 different Greek forms of *fear* result in over 150 biblical references. In specific assurances, God's people are encouraged not to be afraid of death, disease, storms, pestilence, war, armies, enemies, false prophets, announcements of angels, the resurrected Jesus, other people, or God. God's chosen ones worship God with "fear and trembling." When it comes to God's punishment or vengeance, at some times God's people should be fearful and at other times not fearful.

The first words spoken by leaders and prophets when they face fearful circumstances are often, "Do not be afraid." This frequent comforting command, sometimes spoken by angels, prefigures what neuroscience would later discover, that spoken words, especially those shared in loving conversation, quickly help dissipate fear.

Three references summarize fear's presence in the Bible. The first, the words of Job's friend Elihu, puts "fear of God" in perspective. "So we humans fear God, because he shows no respect for those who are proud and think they know so much" (Job 37:24 CEV). The second offers Jesus' wisdom, contrasting fear of people with fear of God. "My friends, don't be afraid of people. They can kill you, but after that, there is nothing else they can do. God is the one you must fear. Not only can he take your life, but he can throw you into hell. God is certainly the one you should fear!" (Luke 12:4-5 CEV). The third comes from Isaiah and recounts why fear is not necessary. "I am the LORD your God. I am holding your hand, so don't be afraid. I am here to help you" (Isa. 41:13 CEV).

God's wisdom, comfort, and courage so that they can carry out God's will in spite of life's fearful circumstances. Their reciprocal support and protection enable you to be wise, comforted, and courageous.

Nearly a decade ago, psychologist Daniel Goleman wrote about fear-reducing practices. He showed how so-called emotional hijackings—fear and anger taking control of the brain's thought processes—could be thwarted or shortened by simple reconditioning of responses or relearning empathy. Goleman understood that brains captured by raw, destructive emotions could be retrained to think first about others' reactions, and that this emotional intelligence could replace the tripwires of instant, brain-overpowering fear and anger.

Words—and also word-making—contribute to fear reduction. The simple processes of finding and speaking words reset your cerebral cortex, helping it take back its normal functions from your primal fear systems. "Talk to me!" is a favored technique for emergency workers

---

Brain Fact

Face recognition—your brain's ability to immediately identify and understand the faces of others—seems to be a special function of specific cells in the amygdala. A lack of face recognition capability, sometimes evident in stroke or other brain damage, is called *proscopagnosia* (proh-scoh-pag-NOSE-ee-ah), from the Greek words for *face* and *not knowing.*

---

when they want to calm persons who are over-stressed or fearful because of the trauma of an accident or extreme crisis. The same principle works in your brain when you are under the influence of lesser fears. Speech—especially conversation—requires syntax and empathy; both of these obligate many sections of your brain to work together instead of working on fear reactions. Fear is pushed aside when your brain's fear-related circuits instead take up the complex and interrelated brain functions involved in speech.

Trying It Out

Imagine yourself engaged in a normal worship experience with others. In your mental journey through a liturgy or order of worship, stop at all the places where fear-reduction could possibly occur. Examine each stopping place with a grateful heart to God. Where does God's love pour out? Where do you show love, engage in conversation, or speak comforting words together with others? Where do you touch other worshipers? Where do you find assurances of forgiveness, safety, or well-being? How do joy or laughter ripple through the congregation around you? When are your legitimate fears named or sins confessed? Where in worship are God's mercy, power, kindness, or gifts made evident or bestowed on you?

One kind of speech that works especially well as a fear-reducer is conversation. Because conversation is a social act, your brain synchronizes itself with the brains of others around you, who may not be as fearful as you. Loving or empathic conversation reintroduces feel-good neurotransmitters into your brain where cortisol and adrenaline were previously determining how your brain would react. Conversation invokes your brain's social intelligence, a collection of higher-order functions that require more complex, whole-brain activity. Because more of your brain's functions are required for conversation, fear has literally less brain space in which to work, and so is diminished.

Brain Fact

The brain's funny bone is the medial ventral pre-frontal cortex. Phonological jokes—puns intended—also involve the right temporary lobe. Humor is serious work for your brain, because it integrates your capabilities for inference, self-awareness, and emotional and physical responses in order to release tension or bring pleasure.

Laughter is a proven fear reducer, most likely because it's a pleasurable substitute for fear-based emotions. Laughter and humor help dissipate fear because they relax your body. In laughter, the parasympathetic system—rest and digest are among its functions—increases its activity and produces positive emotions such as happiness and contentment. Because laughter involves both your body and brain, it serves as worthy competition to fear and its associated emotions.

Perhaps the best short-term biological fear-reducers can be found in the three normal fear responses the brain sets in motion immediately: fighting, fleeing, and freezing. Your fear diminishes once the source of that fear is:

- Eliminated—because you fought, the danger was "killed."
- Left behind—because you fled, the danger was left in the dust.
- No longer present—because you froze, the "dangerous predator" lost interest.

Although it might seem overly optimistic or trite, perfect love casts out fear. The neurotransmitters of love are powerful substitutes for brain chemicals involved in fear, anger, anxiety, and stress. Because love's expression includes both touch and conversation, your entire body is engaged in giving and receiving love, making love a formidable adversary to fear. You follow Christ and live by his example. You know his life story. You know that love in action ultimately triumphs over almost every negative human emotion, fear included.

Finally, a dependable way to manage fear is to avoid situations in which you feel helpless or vulnerable. If that's not possible, try to maintain an attitude of positive control and optimism about the situation. One example of this attitude comes from the field of asset-based planning. In this way of thinking, problems can also be viewed as useful in some way, thus losing some of their power to induce fear.

Brain Fact

In the brain, love consists of attraction and attachment. The attraction stage may be associated with an increase of an amphetamine-related chemical, phenylethylamine (fen-ihl-eh-THIGH-lah-meen) (PEA) and lasts between eighteen months and three years. Attachment, a more mellow phase of love, is associated with the neurotransmitters serotonin, oxytocin, and vasopressin. It can last a lifetime.

Dealing with Fear in Your Congregation

Now that you know about some effective fear-reducers, let's take some time to think about specific steps you might take to keep fear from harming your congregation. Consider these starter ideas and add to them from your own experience.

1. Admit fear exists, almost everywhere and in almost everyone. The first step in combating any problem is to name it. Don't let fear hide behind its secondary effects.
2. Confess your own fears, especially those that have become familiar, habituated, or even comfortable. As they continue in your life, fears can become sins, especially as they harm others or the enterprises of the Holy Spirit.
3. Use fear-reducing mantras regularly. "What am I afraid of here?" is a good one. So is "Don't be afraid."

4. Before fearsome situations occur, analyze what might be truly dangerous and what might be true opportunity.

5. Put "good" into the Good News. Start with the question, "What's so good about 'the Good News'"? If you can't describe how God's action in Christ Jesus makes life good, stop what you're doing and spend some time rereading Jesus' teachings.

6. Insert fear-allaying behaviors and ideas into meeting agendas, congregational events, programs, and communications. For example, where does loving touch happen in your congregation's life together? Yes, I'm aware of the greeting of peace during worship, but where else?

7. When you sense that others are fearful, stop moving through your agenda, your message, or your objectives and deal with the fear you sense. An especially important place to do this is when people are afraid of you, or vice versa.

8. Investigate and use practical fear-reducing planning approaches such as asset mapping. See Luther Snow's *The Power of Asset Mapping* (The Alban Institute, 2004) for specific techniques and solid philosophical and theological background for this time-tested way of leading congregations past fear towards concerted action.

9. Replace fearful leaders (yes, including yourself) if they can't be led past their self-poisoning attitudes and behaviors. One way to talk about the necessary change is to say, "Friend, if you continue to live with high levels of fear, anger, or anxiety, your physical, mental, and spiritual health are at risk."

10. Don't honor or accept decisions based solely on ill-placed fears or anger. Instead, excuse yourself from the process or speak against the emotional hijacking that has led to the decision.

11. If fear is especially prevalent in your congregation, plan a leaders' retreat that deals specifically with the subject. Explore the theology and physiology of fear and all its components. In prayer and personal covenants with each other, agree how you will work together to lessen the impact of fear in your life together.

12. Identify the most and least fearful leaders (or members) of your congregation. Set up a series of monthly breakfast conversations to talk

fearlessly together about your congregation's vitality or future directions.

```
┌─────────────────────────────────────────────────────── ? ─┐
│                      Big Question                          │
│ Just in case the question has been building in your mind, what *are* you going │
│ to do about all the fear in your congregation, including your own? │
└────────────────────────────────────────────────────────────┘
```

Opportunity Goes to Church

Danger and fear aren't the only choices when your brain encounters the church. Opportunity may also show up in your congregation, with a different set of results.

Remember that the danger and opportunity choice starts at an unconscious, prethinking level in your brain. Once you have chosen danger, the mechanisms of fear kick in. When your brain unconsciously determines that opportunity is present, a different set of conscious behaviors ensue. As with primal fear, the first reactions to opportunity are quickly followed by more careful analyses of the input, more connections between sections of the brain and perhaps more careful thoughts about consequences.

Whether your brain ultimately determines that it faces danger or an opportunity, its goal is the same: survival. The danger and opportunity decision is an entirely practical one. In other words, in some situations your brain determines that danger is present and fear is the most practical response. At other times, an opportunity choice is in the best interest of the brain or body.

My aim here is to ask you to consider how the most important quality of opportunity-choices in the church might be their usefulness over time. To say this another way, when you choose opportunity over danger, you may be making the most practical choice in the long run. Although danger-based fear could be helpful in the short-run, its long-term effects work against your congregation's health and the health of leaders like you.

So then, how and when *does* the opportunity as brain choice show up in your congregation? Your brain—and your congregation as brain—are probably choosing opportunity rather than fear when you:

- Bathe risk-laden decisions in joy and hope rather than a grim determination to survive.
- Take all the time you need, when under duress, to make important decisions.
- Use asset-based approaches for planning, instead of needs-based or problem-solving techniques.
- Feel good about your decisions, and are energized to carry them to completion.
- React to almost every situation with an attitude of pragmatic abundance-counting rather than pessimistic assessment of your deficits.
- See possibilities inside your problems or needs.
- Think long term rather than short term.
- Tip slightly toward "Gospel" in the eternal Law and Gospel tension.
- Use the question, "What's useful here?" as the start of decision-making and planning processes.
- Make "possible opportunity" your default choice.
- Readily admit failures, and learn from them.

Questions and Conjectures

Let me finish the chapter with a few curiosities that have occurred to me over the years. Some of my interests show up here as questions, others as tentative hypotheses.

Who "Wins" in Fear-Filled Situations?

The simple answer, at least for the long-term, is no one. Because danger-choosing and reactive fear can become habits, their physically and mentally harmful effects will eventually reveal themselves—on you personally and on your congregation as a whole. Individual and congregational immune systems will be comprised. Over-taxed parts of the body will eventually collapse or lose their effectiveness. Fear will become a primary cause for leader burnout. Those who continually warn of wolves will soon lose their audience. If you or your congregation continue to live with self-perpetuating fear, the eventual end of that behavior will be death of one kind or the other.

So who would want to win by continually identifying situations as danger-filled, by being fearful, or by causing fear? The most cynical answer may be the most correct: those who want to obtain short-term gain by using techniques guaranteed to capture the minds of others. Some political and religious leaders purposely engage in fear-mongering because they know how quickly fear gathers people's attention and energy. Manipulative leaders can easily control their followers by regularly stimulating them with warnings of danger or with fear-inducing messages.

How Is Fear the Default Position of Our Present-day Culture?

At the time of this writing—and most likely at the time of your reading—fear is the predominant emotion in world governments and enterprises of all kinds. Anything and anyone is now potentially dangerous—from overseas travel to immigrants from the Middle East to those who dare criticize the government. Because fear quickly motivates people to action, it is an efficient tool for mobilizing people to buy and sell barely useful products, to take up arms against infidels, or to dispose of a pastor. Powerful people and organizations have a vested interested in keeping the general population perpetually locked in fear.

When you and other leaders relate to each other and to congregation members, most likely you're dealing with people already surrounded by real or imagined danger, already prone towards fear.

"Fear Not!" May Be the Church's Most Important Message

"Spreading the Gospel" is a nice phrase, but what does it mean in dangerous and fearful times? In your congregation, "Do not be afraid" could come out like this:

- "This is one place you don't have to be afraid."
- "Afraid of the dark? We can help."
- "We work for the God who beat fear."
- "Fear dump located on our premises."
- "Fear forgiven here."

However you say it, just say it. God doesn't want you to be afraid all of the time, about everything. There is another to way to face life, and it starts with God's love in Christ Jesus.

"Life's Ultimate Fear" Has No Power.

You guessed it—and yes, I saved this for the last—life's ultimate fear is the fear of death. It shows up everywhere. Fear of death likely drives materialism and its underlying cause: basic selfishness. Also related to fear of death are the fear of getting old and fear of getting deathly ill. These fears combine to scare some people into premature divorces, red sports cars, plastic surgery, "cures" for baldness, and overconsumption of nonessential pharmaceutical remedies. In the church, these fears may show up as mindless bleatings about growth or subtle disregard for congregations filled with mostly older members.

Regardless of its reactive behaviors, fear of death has no power over people God has rescued from sin and death. (Yes, that would be you.) Like the people you serve in your congregation, you know that your life is not your own, and that its supposed ending is just a portal to a new beginning. The proof of death's feckless nature is Jesus Christ's triumph over death and death-dealing people. Death is no longer dangerous. As you put into practice what you believe about eternal life through Christ, fear of death has no fangs, no sting, no power over your brain.

Looking Ahead

In the next chapter you get to spend time examining one more brain matter: learning and memory. Before you begin, however, get ready for your reading by asking, "How do you know what you know?"

Exploring Further

With a small group of people, examine any of the following questions or try some of the suggested activities. Make up your own follow-up activities or adapt what you read here.

1. Find a section of this chapter that seemed like it was written with you in mind. What name would you give the section? Why?
2. What part of this chapter could you copy and paste into the next agenda of a meeting at your congregation? What would you hope to accomplish by doing that?
3. What do you know about danger and opportunity that differs from what you read in this chapter?
4. Play around in a printed or online Bible concordance (a listing of Bible passages by word or phrase) to see the various places in the Bible where "fear" or "fear not" occur. How would you summarize what you've found?
5. What questions does this chapter raise but not answer? Where will you go to find good answers?
6. Talk about how this chapter condemns and comforts you as a leader. How can you tell the difference?
7. What do you want to do next, about your fears or your courage?

Chapter 5

Sorting the Mess

Learning and Memory

"EVERYTHING'S PRETTY MUCH A MESS." This may have been the message the Spirit of God brought back after "brooding on the face of the waters" (Gen. 1:2 KJV). Although the initial chaos of creation was itself the work of God's hand—and therefore as "good" as the latter stages of creation— God decided not to let chaos continue into eternity. Eventually God ordered the roiling waters into cogent, discernible places. Eventually God separated light from dark, land from seas, and bright lights from even brighter ones. By God's creating word, living creatures came into being, including humans. When God's first ordering of God's good creation was finished, the mess was sorted.

In this first story of the Bible, created chaos eventually yielded to created order. Since order followed chaos, order took its place as the presumptive default state of the world. Order is most likely the state of affairs that you prefer for your brain and your congregation. Although your brain's activities constitute

---

Brain Fact

You can think of your brain's activity as a complex (or chaotic) system. Chaos is not random activity, however. Chaotic systems are finely tuned to react to random activity, but their self-organizing behaviors indicate an underlying order, however difficult it may be to measure or describe.

---

an essentially chaotic system, your brain self-orders itself through what we call learning and memory. In this chapter, these are the subjects I'll sort through, seeing how they operate in your individual brain as well as the brain that is your congregation.

Big Picture: What Is Learning and Memory?

In this chapter, I'll be using the terms *learning* and *memory* to mean something deeper and more prevalent than merely how you acquire and retain information in an educational setting. It may be helpful to take the terms to a more basic, even neurobiological definition. Let me try that here.

Trying It Out

How do you know what you know? This question invites you to examine the processes by which you sort knowledge, to think about your thinking. Try asking the question after encountering any statement of fact. After you've practiced the question in your own thinking, see how it works to help others improve their thinking capabilities.

First let me admit a small frustration that I experience as a writer: both learning and memory are far more complex than present-day neurobiology can adequately explain. You can understand many of the fascinating mechanisms of memory and learning at both the macro level of brain structures and at the micro level of individual cells. At the macro level you can characterize these two brain (and congregation) functions—learning and memory—as changed behaviors or acquired knowledge, skills, and attitudes. At the micro level, learning and memory occur as changes in individual neurons or congregation members. There is a vast middle (muddled?) ground between macro and micro, however, where we just don't really know what's happening. We may be able to measure infinitely small changes in cell chemistry as neurons learn, but we don't know the processes by which the individual cells in your brain eventually form complex systems of brain matter that result in, say, the ability to read and understand this complex sentence.

That being said, how might you characterize learning and memory as they occur in your brain? I'll give you some choices; we can raise questions about the helpfulness or accuracy of each. In biological terms, you could think of learning and memory as:

- **Changes in brain states.** The presence of an aroused state of mind—as contrasted with a quiescent state of mind—indicates that the brain is learning, forming memories, or recalling memories. Learning involves the attentive (foreground) and memory-sorting functions of the brain, while the monitoring (automatic or background) functions of the brain allow memory-formation. In your congregation, learning is any change in your collective state of mind from despairing to hopeful. What causes *those* "states of mind" to form, given all the other choices?
- **An increase in the number and excellence of neuronal connections.** In this framing of learning and memory, learning could be simply an increase in synaptic connections and memory the efficiency by which the electrical or chemical energy bundles cross synapses. In your congregation, learning could happen when increasing numbers of members converse with each other (Could conversation be a kind of congregational synapse?) and memory could happen when those conversations become collegial decisions at a meeting. Do both memory and learning depend primarily on the speed or number of synapses (or conversations)?
- **The enlargement or reduction of certain brain areas.** If you understand learning and memory in this way, you measure the changes in the size of brain areas devoted to specific functions. Enlarged areas indicate where your brain has learned or remembered a specific skill or capacity. In your congregation, this definition of learning shows up as the amount of building space or financial resources you devote to various ministries or functions of the congregation. How certain are you that any one area of your brain (one group in your congregation) is devoted only to any one function (congregational activity)?
- **Changing boundaries between brain areas that control specific functions.** Learning and memory are seen here in the relative shape

of brain regions, or how areas traditionally assigned to particular functions have overlapped. The more overlapping, the more interrelated the brain's various functions, and the more integrated the learning or memory. In your congregation, this way of thinking about learning and memory show up as intergenerational events or multipurpose programs. Is the shape of an area of the brain—and therefore its boundaries—always an indication of intent (learning and memory), or could boundaries change by chance?

Big Question

Which of these definitions of *learning* and *memory* are closest to your view of the two ideas? How did you come to that choice, and how would you explain your reasons for choosing? And if you couldn't choose, why might that be true?

- **Cell pruning and cell growth.** Recalling chapter 2, you'll remember that your brain chooses to maintain an optimum number of active, efficient neurons, and that repeated neuronal firings result in new cell growth. (Use it or lose it.) In this way of thinking, learning and memory are shaped by the death of some cell groups and the birth or growth of other cell groups. In your congregation, learning and memory are determined by the number of inactive individuals you subtract from your rolls, or the new individuals you add to your congregation-as-brain. Doesn't this make learning and memory into a mechanistic or deterministic matter, one tinged with perhaps more emphasis on accountability?
- **The maturation of reactive brain functions into automatic functions.** Here, learning denotes the moment when a reactive (attention-requiring) brain pattern finally shifts into a more automatic brain pattern (memory-requiring). For example, you have finally learned how to ride a bike when bike riding becomes automatic—when procedural memory ensures the proper operation of this two-wheeled marvel. In your congregation, you could identify learned members as those who are highly loyal to the mission of your congregation, contribute time and money regularly, and exhibit

so-called marks of discipleship. A learned congregation—perhaps not ever achievable in the overall scheme of things—would be one in which all major functions occurred more-or-less automatically, driven by the memory of what should be happening now. Wouldn't this definition make learning and memory always incomplete?

Whichever description of learning and memory you choose, each can be helpful in some ways and problematic in others. The tension between helpful and problematic can also remind you that learning and memory comprise a wonderfully complex set of activities in your brain.

But let's get back to "What are they?" kinds of questions about learning and memory. John Ratey, author of *A User's Guide to the Brain: Perception, Attention and the Four Theaters of the Brain*, defines learning and memory in a functional way. Learning can be thought of as an act that is eventually carried out because it depends on a memory of plans that have already been formulated and rehearsed. In Ratey's way of thinking, actions in the past, present, and future join together with past, present, and future memories.

You've noticed already, I hope, that learning and memory seem to depend on each other, which makes interrelated definitions more correct than definitions that treat one or the other separately. Another unitized definition of learning and memory that might be helpful for you: in learning, current and remembered knowledge is converted into action; you manipulate knowledge about previously acquired knowledge. In your congregation, you might see intertwined learning and memory in members who know your congregation's history and remain active in your congregation's life.

Long-term Potentiation

The biological key to learning and memory may be long-term potentiation (LTP), the innate capability of individual neurons and groups of neurons to develop preferred firing patterns. Here's how LTP works in your brain:

- Every time groups of cells fire in your brain, the synapses in some neurons are strengthened (increasing amounts of neurotransmitters are present) or weakened (decreasing amounts of these same chemicals). The patterns of those strengthenings and weakenings are the beginnings of your memories. Your brain's ability to make those patterns is called LTP.

- These patterns would soon disappear if LTP was not a feature of cell cooperation. Because of LTP, some of your synapses become more strongly connected with others, and the chemical coding among the cells bonds them together. A neuronal pathway has been formed, and now the memory is chemically more likely to occur, and less likely to fade quickly.

- When a new stimulus occurs, neuronal firing patterns use the already existing neuronal highways. The new stimulus is integrated into the patterns, which are now even stronger.

Brain Fact

For some single cell research on LTP, neuroscientists depend on the nerve cells of *Aplysia californica* (aah-plih-SEE-ah cal-ih-FORN-ih-cah), otherwise known as the sea slug. This blob with ears has very large—and easily examined—nerve cells, and only a small number (20,000) compared to the 100 billion nerve cells of the human brain.

- The more the patterns are repeated, the more easily they will be chosen by your brain. The more the patterns are repeated, the more permanent the messages become. Learning occurs because of LTP.

In your congregation, LTP shows up as behaviors that are repeated automatically. "The Annual Persimmon Pie Festival," "The 25th Annual CROP Walk," or the generic "We've always done it that way before"—all are examples of how the already familiar neuronal pathways of your congregation-as-brain are easily engaged and repeated.

Interrelationships among Learning, Memory, and Movement

It's difficult to talk about learning and memory without mentioning their connection to movement, literally and figuratively. (To help you understand the idea of movement, I've included at the end of this chapter a bonus section about the subject.) Learning and memory form a mutually reinforcing loop in your brain. Learning helps information cross from perception into your memory; in turn, your stored memories enable further learning.

When you add movement into this biological system, the interrelationships are fascinating. Physical activity increases your capability for mastering and remembering new information, and new information helps you master and remember physical activity. When I talk to pastors and lay leaders about the physical act of distributing bread and wine at Holy Communion, I am always amazed at the deep spiritual insights— "We are beggars, all of us"—that seem to be triggered by the seemingly simple act of placing food into the outstretched hands of worshipers.

You've seen this idea earlier in this book, written as twin maxims: "What you can imagine, you can do" and "What you can do, you can imagine." How does that work biologically? The same motor circuits that make movement possible can also imagine (or remember?) that movement. This is why sports coaches use imaging techniques to help athletes excel. When imaging is a part of praying, you can participate in the answering of your prayers for changes in the world or changes in your attitudes.

Movement requires you to review, rehearse, and progress through ordered processes to achieve a goal that is observable and measurable. With learning and memory, you focus these processes on ideas or ideals instead of physical activity. Experimental evidence seems consistent; general success or skill in coordinated physical activity correlates with success or skill in mental processes such as reasoning and verbal expression. One of my all-time favorite adages about learning (and social change) is, "Act your way into thinking." When you apply this saying to congregational movement, you

Brain Fact

Individuals who have been blind since birth also use hand gestures when speaking. This may indicate that this way of communicating is hardwired in the brain. Another possibility: That gestures are fundamental to the thinking that accompanies speaking, perhaps both reflecting that thinking or facilitating it.

might be explaining why, over the past several decades, mission trips among high-school students have resulted in increased congregational sensitivity to social justice and world hunger.

Learning, memory, and motion are also interdependent because some motor skills make learning possible—speech or hand gestures, for example. As they find their way into your working or long-term memory, those motor skills become automatic, thus enabling your brain to attend more closely to what you are learning. In your congregation, you can concentrate on the meaning and value of new hymns only after you've sung them for awhile—a complex physical act—and they become familiar.

Some physical activities (sports such as long-distance running, soccer, or tennis) require extensive mental activity. Physical exercise changes the physical chemistry of your brain, allowing or enabling clearer or more creative thinking. Your ability to retrieve memories may be enhanced by the amount of physical activity in which you engage. Motor development in infants correlates positively with their readiness for reading and writing.

Big Question

Preachers, what might happen if your listeners stood up and walked around while you preached? Or if they imagined themselves walking around while you preached?

Physical challenge and feedback are essential features of coordinated physical activity. The substantia nigra (sub-STAN-see-uh NEE-grah), part of the basal ganglia in your midbrain, is critically involved in the feedback process. This structure helps your brain "self-reference," to execute internal cross-checks about what is happening in reference to what just happened and what will happen next. This brain activity is important in both physical activity and learning processes.

Two Kinds of Memory (and Learning)

When you talk about memory, you're actually speaking about a variety of mental processes, about different kinds of memory and learning. Let's look at a few, first at two large categories—short-term and long-term memory—and then at several loosely defined kinds of memory.

Your brain divides memory into two discrete but connected processes: short-term (or working) memory and long-term memory.

Working memory is like the random access memory (RAM) in a computer, momentarily holding the information you are working with. For example, the words I'm typing into my computer right now go into RAM (short-term memory) before I save them onto a hard drive (long-term memory). When the computer is shut off, the short-term memory is gone, reset, and ready for the next task. The long-term memory remains available.

Long-term memory takes up where short-term memory leaves off. After a period of hours, during which time short-term memories consolidate, your cortex sends the collected short-term memory to the hippocampus. The working memory now makes the transition to long-term memory, where it is available for future action and learning.

Short-term (Working) Memory

Working memory allows you both to register current events and retrieve information from long-term memory, while at the same time holding or sending the new information to the right place. Working (or short-term) memory operates in the past (retrieving information from long-term memory) and the present (registering current events) for the purpose of anticipating what will happen next. Past, present, and future blend together in working memory.

Sensory memory, a kind of short-term memory, is your almost-instantaneous and continuous awareness of your sensory input. At every waking moment, you recall separately the cues from your sensory organs—eyes, ears, skin, nose, mouth—and then consolidate them together as a singular experience. You trust sensory memory because it is easily verified and because it's repeated regularly throughout your life experience.

Long-term Memory

By definition, long-term memory is available to your brain long after short-term memory has diminished or disappeared. Long-term memory operates both unconsciously and consciously. Scientists divide long-term memory into three categories: procedural (skills), declarative (facts), and emotional (feelings).

Procedural Memory

You unconsciously recall motor processes in an ordered progression, and replicate those patterned skills on demand. Your procedural memory helps you process, routinize, and recall gross and fine-muscle movements. Procedural memory may also include automatic mental "movements" such as problem-solving. Procedural memory depends on the input and coordination of your senses and feedback mechanisms that detect and correct spatial and motion-sequencing errors. When you engage procedural memory, both your right and left hemispheres work together. In your congregation, you use procedural memory every time you make the sign of the cross, distribute the elements of Holy Communion, or participate in a bell choir.

Brain Fact

The cerebellum (sehr-uh-BELL-uhm) coordinates both physical movement and the movement of thoughts. The cerebellum integrates information and decides when to process information.

Declarative Memory

Your brain consciously processes factual information, including the names and locations of objects and people in their context. Declarative memory includes both episodic (memories of personal experience) and semantic memory (memories of cultural knowledge). Each of the varieties of declarative memory requires associations with time, space, and emotional contexts.

All factual memories are tied to their contexts. Take the visual form of declarative memory, for example. You recall the shape and spatial orientation of objects you have seen, and recognize those objects from any angle. Amazingly, your brain holds and adds information about an object even when only part of it is visible. In your congregation, the visual form of declarative memory may show itself in the personal meanings you derive from the rich array of visual symbols (for example, artifacts, icons, the sign of the cross, or the cross itself) displayed or used in your congregation's life together.

Episodic Memory. You put facts and events into their place in time so that you can freely recall the entire episode. Episodic memory is the stuff of autobiographical storytelling or legacies. When freely shared across generations, episodic memory keeps you from disdaining the past, an attitude that makes you vulnerable to repeat the mistakes of your forebears. Episodic memory is the heart of much of the witness of Scripture—stories passed from mouth to ear over many generations by people who were awed by God. Episodic memory prospers in your congregation because it carries forward the blessings you have received from the past into the lives of those who will follow you. Episodic memory shows up in congregational self-studies (for example, before you call a new pastor), pastoral counseling, personal stories in sermons, congregational histories, annual meetings, times when leadership is transferred, and in new member orientation processes.

Brain Fact

The brain's sense of place—also called spatial orientation—may be located primarily in the hippocampus. This seahorse-shaped structure remembers the regularities of life, including one's sense of place. The hippocampus maps the brain's experiences in a specific place as a memorable event.

Semantic Memory. You recall facts and everyday functions free from the subjectivity of personal experience, and you're able to group those facts into useful categories. Semantic memory is at the heart of language—grammar, word meanings, and syntax—and more reliable than subjective episodic memory. Semantic memory places you in a particular culture. In your congregation, semantic memory shows up in your constitution and bylaws, knowing the Ten Commandments, knowing where the costumes for the Christmas pageant are stored, instruction in doctrine or formal Bible interpretation, and the keeping and reporting of statistics about your congregation.

Emotional Memory

Because your brain's amygdala marks incoming information with emotional tags, it makes sense that your brain's emotional memory is a vital key to activating attention and to holding together long-term memory. If declarative memory is about remembering what happened, emotional memory is about how you felt about what happened.

Emotional memories can key your brain to enlist other kinds of memory. For example, your memory of how you felt when you first kissed someone you loved may be the trigger to help you recall where and when that happened (episodic memory).

Emotional memories are powerful and long-lasting, perhaps because they involve more areas of the brain or because emotions themselves are a core component of being human.

Trying It Out

Think back to your early years and the kinds of memory you took advantage of. When you were an infant, your brain first gained the ability for procedural memory (and learning). You may have learned, for example, the simple physical routine of folding your hands for bedtime prayer. Next came declarative (factual) memory—you learned and used the names of people, objects, and activities for which to pray. Semantic memory activated procedural memory: your automatic nightly routine may have started with the verbal cue, "It's time to pray!" Eventually you gained enough episodic memory to recall specific, time-sequenced sets of experiences. In these episodic stories you found the content for your prayers. And now, even after all these years, you still remember the entire sequence of prayer mini-events at bedtime as part of a familiar—and emotionally desirable—routine that signals the start of nighttime sleep (emotional memory).

Language

Language is a subset of semantic memory. You use language—naming and arranging words in syntax—to obtain quick access to the vast stores of memories you have collected throughout your life. Because meaning is embedded in words, language memory activates other types of memory. Think, for example, what would happen if I asked you to recall your first experience with God's presence. Besides finding the words to express your feelings (an emotional memory) at that moment, your brain would most likely call on declarative memory (where you were at the moment and what your senses told you at that moment) to enrich the full-blown memory of this important event in your life. In that example, words alone would not have been sufficient, but your language memory could have triggered other, useful forms of memory.

Language memory is an important—and efficient—variety of semantic memory in your congregation-as-brain. In rites and rituals, constitutions and the record of meetings, reports and oft-told stories, sermons and meditations, newsletters and inserts in worship bulletins— in each of these cases, language is being used for acquiring new knowledge *and* as an efficient way of remembering the elements that make up your congregation's continuing health. Creeds are the distilled memories of theological truth; confessing them, one to another, is a way of reinstalling centuries-old memories into your congregation's brain, as well as a way of proclaiming who you are. Learning and memorizing formulaic spiritual utterances (such as prayers, mantras, or Scripture passages) helps you take advantage of the power of language.

Learning Styles

The varieties of memory and learning give your brain choices of how to learn, according to what educators call preferred learning styles. Because all the varieties of memory are interrelated, it may be true that once your brain finds one way to take in information it then has access to other kinds of memory. This phenomenon may be like a home with several entrances, each of which leads to the entire house and to the other entrances.

Your congregation-as-brain may also have a preferred style of learning (and memory). Event-based programming (procedural, episodic, and emotional memory) may excite the majority of your congregation's members. Or word-based activities (sermons, present-and-discuss group experiences) might energize the members whose memory and learning most favor semantic memory and language. The most likely scenario about learning styles, of course, is that your congregation's members prefer all of the styles, in varying degrees and at various times. When it comes to learning, no one method or activity appeals to all participants, so you have the responsibility to use a variety of methods by which the people you serve can grow in faith and love for God's world. Paul might have had a similar idea in mind when he explained to the Corinthians, "I have become all things to all people, that I might by all means save some" (1 Cor. 9:22 NRSV).

An Important Digression: Learning Language

Take a little side trip with me. This digression is about how we learn language. If your congregation doesn't help members acquire spiritual language, your congregation's memory will be severely limited. A group of people without memory are not destined to live long.

The language functions of your brain are distributed around your entire brain, which may mean that language organizes your brain and its memories like no other brain activity. (Psycholinguists express the idea this way: "As you speak, write, or hear, so you think.")

Your language learning (and memory) began *in utero,* with the sounds you heard (and remembered) coming from outside the womb. When you were as young as eight months old, you could begin hearing the differences between phonemes and the beginning and endings of words and sentences. In your first two months of life, crying and grunting were your language. By about your third month you began cooing and laughing. Somewhere between the fifth to seventh month of your life, you started distinguishing between vowels and consonants, and began babbling in syllables. By the time you reached your 10-month milestone in life, you were grouping phonemes into the syllables specific to the language of your ethnic environment. Between 12 and 18 months old, you started using words and phrases, but couldn't quite put them into grammatically correct constructs. By the time you were two to three years old, you were speaking in complete sentences and your hearing and speaking vocabularies increased. In the following years, you increased the length of the sentences you used, increased in skill with more complicated syntax, and solved the problems of verb tenses and singular and plural forms of nouns. Somewhere between your third and seventh year of life you began to read and write, using both your language skills and your language memory. If you were fortunate through these years of development to have parents and loved ones who spoke with you, read to you, and listened to you, your vocabulary grew to a significant size, perhaps helping you develop skills in reasoning and problem-solving.

Brain Fact

The brains of children ages three to ten consume twice as much glucose (sugar) as the brains of adults. This difference may be due to the relative inefficiency of children's brains, and to the fact that they are forming colossal numbers of brand-new neuronal connections. Young learning brains need to be fed.

The analogous conclusion I want you to draw from this discussion is that you must find the people, money, time, and passion that will help children, and individuals new to Christianity, to gradually develop the spiritual language(s) they will need to form memorable relationships with their God and with each other through life. The privilege and responsibility to accomplish this task rests squarely on your shoulders as leader.

Problems with Memory

Memories are not always available for recall. One controversial example is called traumatic amnesia, in which a frightful event or situation—such as rape, armed conflict, or childhood abuse—may temporarily (or permanently) preclude a memory from becoming available for your brain's foreground attention. Continuing physical pain also may deprive your brain of its ability to learn, or to form and retrieve memories.

Working memory becomes dysfunctional when it is overloaded with storage-ready information. For example, people with attention deficit disorders may find it difficult to shut out the noise of competing inputs, and therefore not be able to remember what may not have entered their short-term memory in the first place. For a treatment of this subject in-depth, especially the intriguing notion that congregations themselves may suffer from attention deficit disorders, see Gary Peluso-Verdend's *Paying Attention: Focusing Your Congregation on What Matters* (The Alban Institute, forthcoming).

In old age, forgetting is a function of the slower speed of the aging brain. The capabilities of some elderly persons to store and retrieve information may decrease because of a decline in the available stores of dopamine, some atrophying of neurons, decreased blood flow, and decreased glucose metabolism in the frontal lobes. Decreased use of brain capacity is also a factor in slowing down the aging brain.

Brain Fact

Chronic pain may be far more harmful to human brains than was thought less than a decade ago. Besides often leading to depression or anxiety, chronic pain can physically shrink your brain. The atrophy of nerve cells, primarily in the prefrontal cortex, can result in poor judgment skills. Fifty-seven percent of people in the United States reported chronic or recurring pain in the past year.

Memories are not certain or infallible. False memories can be the result of the power of suggestion. When they are repeated over time, states of high emotion of any kind can diminish or destroy memory and memory-making capabilities. At a cellular level, memories are never exact because the neurons that rearrange themselves as encoded memories are transferred from short- to long-term memory. Your brain interprets and rewires all memories almost immediately after you perceive an event.

Your congregation probably has problems with its memory, too. Older congregations can slow down—"decreased blood" flow is analogous to the decreasing energy of members—or take longer to make decisions. Chronic pain—the lasting effects of conflict, clergy sexual misconduct, sudden tragedy, or continuing despair—can limit your congregation's capacity to remember accurately or hopefully. If you are constantly energized with new programs, new ideas, or new leaders, your congregation's neurons may be so busy constantly rewiring circuits—new committees, new program titles, new grand plans—that their memories of the past are not accurate anymore. Like many congregations, yours may also be overwhelmed with information—from denominational staff, vendors of congregational services and products, or the long lines of complainers—that your working memory takes a backseat to dealing with all this information.

Big Question

How would you rate your congregation's learning and memory skills, attitudes, or knowledge? How do you know?

Learning and Memory in the Scriptures

The Bible is like the church's long-term memory system, a trusted and readily available storehouse of information from God about God, useful for individual believers and entire congregations. You might think of the Bible as the long-term storage space for several kinds of memory, including the following:

- **Sensory.** The Bible remembers what the church's senses have discovered over and over, so that you are continuously aware of the stinking reality of evil, the strong, warm hug of love, the brightness of hope, the musical sounds of forgiveness.
- **Episodic Memory.** The careful telling and retelling of the collected stories of God's gracious acts has continued over thousands of years. Even though those spoken words have been written into the Bible, the tales of God's encounter with humans still persist as powerful memories.
- **Semantic Memory.** For generations, the revered (and regularly forsaken) laws of God were passed on to future generations as semantic memory. The warnings of the prophets called God's people to recall—and obey—their semantic memory of the Law. The passages of Scripture help orient you and your congregation to your role in the world, your place in time, your spot on the larger map of God's intent for all of creation. The words (and Word) of God are available to you and your congregation for ready use in your daily lives. Words

about God's love become your own loving words and deeds. The words and deeds of Christ's life, death, and resurrection save you from death. God's Word or word offers you a redemptive voice when the Accuser (Satan) tries to silence you with false condemnation.

- **Procedural Memory.** In the Scriptures, you and your congregation can find the stored memory of those who have lived before you, who have turned faith, hope, and love into action. The record of their activities helps you gain wisdom and courage for your own activities in God's name. Bundled in various packets of remembered procedures, the passages of Scripture offer you answers to the question, "How, then, shall we live according to God's will?" The Ten Commandments are a prime example.

The whole of the Old Testament is the record of God's mighty acts, written by faithful scribes and storytellers so that no one would forget God's miraculous deliverance, terrifying punishment, or undeserved love. During the Babylonian captivity, a pious group of Jewish leaders—who evolved into the Pharisees of Jesus' time—remembered their language and its function in bonding God's people to God's law, and thence to God.

The New Testament is also a memory-holder about equally mighty acts of God, this time as a record of Jesus' life, and how his followers interpreted Jesus' words and actions. By their written record they enabled countless generations of Jesus' followers to learn and remember what we have not witnessed firsthand.

Wisdom about learning, memory, and movement fills the pages of Scripture. Here are a few examples for your consideration:

- "Parents, don't be hard on your children. Raise them properly. Teach them and instruct them about the Lord" (Eph. 6:4 CEV). In the straightforward language of Paul, an unavoidable word about spiritual learning and memory travels across the centuries: both are the responsibility of parents.
- "You must be very careful not to forget the things you have seen God do for you. Keep reminding yourselves and tell your children and grandchildren as well" (Deut. 6:9 CEV). The memories of parents can and should turn into the learnings of their descendants.

- "Keep your Creator in mind when you are young!" (Eccl. 12:1 CEV). Could "in (your) mind" be translated into neurobiological terms such as "long-term memory"?
- Prophets, kings, poets, proverb-makers, and Gospel writers yearned for ways to help God's people learn and remember. The Ebenezer stone was erected as a memorial to God's miraculous victory over enemies (Josh. 24:27). The ritualized remembrance of the Passover was an antidote to forgetfulness. Christ's followers remembered his words—"Eat this as a way of remembering me" (Luke 24:19 CEV)—and ritualized his forgiving presence as a kind of procedural memory.
- Sensory memory is evident in one of my favorite Scripture passages, "Taste and see that the Lord is good!" (Ps. 34:8 KJV). With just a little thought, I can also find procedural, episodic, and declarative memory in this invitation.

Perhaps the most complete treatment of the subject of learning and memory comes in the candid words of James 1:22-25 (CEV). Please permit my parenthetical comments as I interpret this passage with learning and memory in mind.

Brain Fact

The commonly reproduced "taste map" of the tongue—showing discrete areas of the tongue responsive to particular tastes (such as sweet, sour, salty, and bitter)—is wrong. The map was first printed in the early twentieth century from improperly interpreted research in the 1800s. The facts about taste? The tongue can detect tastes of all kinds anywhere there are taste buds.

"Obey God's message! *(Learn in order to take action.)* Don't fool yourselves by just listening to it. *(False memories occur when only one kind of sensory input is not integrated with other senses.)* If you hear the message and don't obey it, you are like people who stare at themselves in a mirror and forget what they look like as soon as they leave. *(Episodic memory has gone awry, perhaps because it's not connected to action.)* But you must never stop looking at the perfect law *(semantic memory)* that sets you free. God will bless you in everything you do, if you listen and obey *(When procedural memory is correlated to and supported by movement, observable learning takes place.)*, and don't just hear and forget." *(Memory of any kind is preferable to not remembering at all!)*

Learning and Memory Go to Church

Before I begin this section, let me offer you this memory-jogger from the beginning of this chapter. You could describe learning and memory at a reductionistic, single-cell level, and broadly, as acquisition of measurable knowledge, skills, or attitudes. But it's still difficult to know and talk about the middle place between single cells and large systems of thought.

This difficulty occurs in this book's comparison of your brain with your congregation-as-brain. You can hear and understand stories of conversion and life-changing moments in the life of a single congregation member. Over time, you can also see the large-scale changes in a congregation. The mystery is, how can you parse the indescribable middle place, the space between the small (each member as a kind of neuron) and the large (your entire congregation as a kind of brain)? It would be fascinating to track the state of mind of an individual believer as it gradually develops into the state of well-being for the entire congregation.

Memory and learning are basic operations of your brain, and so make their presence felt in almost every structure and function of your congregation-as-brain. Your congregation's vitality depends on its ability to acquire useful information, and to store and retrieve that information when appropriate. These few examples illustrate the necessary functions of learning and memory in your congregation:

- **Refuge.** Even though danger and fear may abound in the world around you, your congregation persists as a place where learning and memory bring order into chaotic lives. Children, youth, and adults learn how to behave as God's people in the world.
- **Worship.** In times of praise and prayer, you remember (or learn for the first time?) that you are *not* God, that you have purpose and meaning in life, that forgiveness washes clean the flawed and selfish

synapses of self-idolatry. The ongoing alleluia of worship circles the world and encompasses all of time as a kind of global memory that never goes away even though it's constantly given away.

- **Legacy.** If sociobiologists are right, one of your most powerful drives is the urge to pass on your genetic coding to the next generation. At an emotional level, this yearning might express itself as your hope that your children carry forward the values and identity of your family. In your congregation-as-brain, the same kind of biological or emotional forces give urgency to your ministry. You're not afraid of dying. Instead, you have received (learned) something valuable— the memories of God's love through history—and you want to ensure that this centuries-long strand of memory—this grand, eons-old "neuron"—extends even farther, into other places and generations.

Brain Fact

For the brain, time may be measured as a kind of tick of the brain's internal clock: the time it takes for a loop of neural activity to be completed, from the substantia nigra (subb-STAN-shee-uh NIGH-grah) at the base of the brain—a place where dopamine is produced—to the prefrontal cortex and back. The average time for this loop to be completed is one-tenth of a second.

- **Re-membering.** By inserting a hyphen, you add to this memory-laden word another important function that your congregation is well equipped to undertake: the re-attaching of people to God and to each other. People who are lost or adrift in life (perhaps they lack an existential version of declarative or emotional memory?) are invited to a place where they belong, where they are included as part of a purposeful body of God's people. As you invite people into the fellowship of your congregation, you offer them God's forgiveness, salvation, and life direction. You also offer them the possibility of storing new memories in their brains!

- **Memory Storage.** Your congregation may excel in learning (such as with good sermons, solid Christian education programs, or a well-written newsletter) and that's good. It's equally important that you maintain equally effective means for the storage of memories in your congregation's life together. For example, committing the congregation's history to only the recapitulation of minutes from coun-

cil meetings—or perhaps worse, the biographies of the congregation's pastoral leadership—leaves out episodic and emotional memory, thus diminishing the impact of full, meaning-laden memory.

Sorting It Out

Although God still moves on the face of the waters in the chaotic
events of these times, you and your God-created brain also have some
responsibility to engage in the sorting process, for the sake of the world.
Perhaps you even have the privilege of adding order to what might seem
to be a mess, in your congregation or even in your own life. Your remembering and learning abilities can help. God's order (coming after God's
chaos) is a gift to be shared with the world, and you are part of the long
line of God's people who offer love where there is hate, hope where there
is despair, forgiveness where there is sin. As you remember God's grace
in your life, you'll be inspired to proclaim—and live—grace wherever
you move. God's Spirit is like that.

> ### Trying It Out
> With a few friends, assess the ways in which the activities of your congrega-
> tion help strengthen the memory-making and memory-storing capabilities
> of members. For example, how do you encourage the story-telling conversa-
> tions of episodic memory? Or how easily can members of your congregation
> access the sensory memory that lies under the semantic memory of your con-
> gregation's history?

Exploring Further

With a small group of people, examine any of the following questions or try some of the suggested activities.

1. Down the left side of a large piece of paper, list the kinds of memory found in this chapter. (Yes, you can add your own categories.)

Now try to find examples of each kind of memory in your congregation's life together. (Hint: start with the ideas in this chapter.)

2. How valuable are your memories? How skilled are you at forming, storing, or retrieving memories? How do you know?

3. Talk about this idea: our job as leaders is to collect and disperse the faith stories (episodic memory) of members, to each other and to our community.

4. How do the ideas of learning and memory help you carry out your role as a leader? Be specific.

5. Play around with the words *learning* and *memory* in your computer's search engine, in a Bible concordance, or in a free-association exercise with a group of people. ("What's the first thing that comes to your mind when I say the word *memory*?")

6. How do you want to be remembered?

7. What part of this chapter's content might change the way you think or behave as a leader? How would the rest of us see the change?

Bonus Section

Movement: A Brain-Based Metaphor for Ecclesiology

Introduction

Some things work best when they follow most everything else. Think, for example, about dessert (after a good meal), Christ the King Sunday (after all of Pentecost), or laughter (after a good story or joke). So, near the end of this book is a little surprise. In the spirit of strawberry shortcake, hymns of praise, and chortling and giggling, I offer you a few extra pages of metaphor-laden thought that might help you reimagine your congregation. Movement offers a metaphor that describes your brain and your church. (That's why the book title, "Your Brain *Goes* to Church" instead of "Your Brain Lives at Church" or "Your Brain Sits Around Church and Does Pretty Much Nothing Else Except Complain.")

What's Movement, Anyhow?

A good place to start is the question, "What's movement all about?" The answers have biological and metaphorical dimensions. In your brain, movement shows up as the following phenomena:

- Billions of atoms in your brain, constantly engaged in erratic and constant movement. The action appears to be random, but may be exquisitely ordered.

- The 40-hertz oscillation (or hum) of brain cells. Back and forth is basic to all of life. Even the stars vibrate.
- Packets of electrical and chemical energy progressing along pathways between and among millions of neurons. The chemicals and the energy move in many directions at once.
- Neurons that grow into specific areas of your brain as you mature. Brain scientists talk about cell migration to describe this activity.
- Bundles of neurons rearranging their firing sequence in order to carry out various functions. The movement: split-second regroupings of vast numbers of brain cells.
- The activity on neuronal highways that your brain first chooses as reliable because of repeated use. Brain scientists call this habituation, but you might think of the movement as a normal commute.
- A three-stage process: analyzing external and internal data, coming up with a response plan, and executing the plan.

Brain Fact

Somatic nerves, also called motor neurons, cause the contraction of muscle cells.

It seems that you could talk about movement in any number of ways, but two major categories emerge: excited oscillation in the same location, and excited progress from one location to another.

Moving Advantages

At a cellular or chemical level, all matter moves—except for inert gases. Large-scale motion, however, is the singular province of ambulatory living things. Plants with roots can move in limited ways—by transforming light, air, water, or dirt into food, growing leaves or flowers, and distributing nutrients—but they spend their lives in one place, dependent on the environment in which they originate.

Along with other organisms that have wings, legs, fins, or other appendages that enable movement, humans have an advantage over other creatures: they can find or create their own food. Not coincidentally, human food consists mainly of nonmoving plants and the slow-moving animals that eat them. Moving creatures, especially humans, have another distinct biological advantage: they can more easily escape becoming food. (As an amateur scientist, I can report reliably that no human has ever been eaten by a rose bush.)

Your brain helps you with movement, enabling the thoughts and words that communicate your intents and needs about movement. Your brain also initiates and coordinates large- and small-muscle movements that are powerful, precise, mindful, and almost always effective. Your legs and arms, your toes and fingers, your sensory organs, and your brain-holding skull—all work together to make you a long-term survivor among other moving beings.

Your moving brain makes moving decisions, and you decide that "there" might be better than "here" (or vice versa). Thus you determine the advantages of opportunity and avoid the disadvantages of danger. Your brain's motor system—motor cortex, basal ganglia, and cerebellum—kick into gear, skeletal muscles coordinate their actions with space-orienting senses (hearing, seeing, smelling) and the movement sequence is completed.

A Moving Portrayal of Your Body

Movement is necessary for the basic functions of your life. Digestion involves the crushing coordination of teeth, jaws, and tongue. Peristaltic movement sends digested food through a system whose end result is called a bowel movement. Respiration requires the repeated contraction and expansion of your chest muscles. Your heart keeps its regular rhythms, harumphing a life-enabling message through a system of pulsating vessels: "Keep that blood moving."

Your body has three movement systems:

1. Your leg and foot system, which enables changes in your physical location.
2. Your arm and hand system, which allows you to grasp, lift, hold, throw, and catch objects of almost any size.
3. Your mouth and throat system, which enables the movement of food into your body, and the rhythmic vibrations of air molecules to create speech.

When you employ these systems with more than a little style, grace, or beauty, the result is called "the arts"—sculpting, painting, dancing, singing, instrumental performance. When competition and political or economic considerations are added in, physical activities become "sports."

Vigorous movement—exercise—is a simple life-assurance policy with low-cost daily premiums, and it partially protects your health. Lack of movement adds weight and problems to your life. "Get more exercise" is at once both a biological necessity and a clue to cure. Learning and memory are dependent on your body's ability to move in small and large ways.

Less movement begets less capability for movement. Your growing incapacity for movement hastens the inevitable end of your body's internal and external movement, namely, death. Casey Stengel might have talked about the idea this way: When you stop moving, you die when you stop moving.

Movement through the Scriptures

In the beginning, the created world was a mess (Gen. 1:2), but the Spirit of God moved over the face of the waters. When only a garden housed the first humans, not much movement was required. Like the plants they tended, Adam and Eve could prosper in a state of God-blessed bliss because of their own virtual rootedness among food-providing plants. Movement—passage out of the garden, the movement of physical labor, the movement of childbirth—became a necessary element of life after Adam and Eve made their own choices about food.

The pilgrim people of the Old Testament—"My father was a wandering Aramean" (Deut. 26:5 RSV)—and the metaphorical sheep of Psalm 23 found comfort and sustenance as they meandered through life under God's protection and guidance. The terrible movement of God's avenging angel among the Egyptians propelled God's people into nomadic life in the Sinai Desert, where they counted on God's cloud- and fire-pillared presence to lead them forward. Jonah moved in the wrong direction and was carried by a large fish in the right direction, toward his God-directed place of personal mission.

Movement typifies parts of the New Testament story as well. In the middle of a taxing trip to Bethlehem, a baby is born and God splits open history so that God's salvation can spread to the world. Sagacious scholars followed the movement—and eventual nonmovement—of a star, ending up at a quiet stable where they were moved to wonder and praise. The three years of Jesus' ministry were characterized by his incessant travel from town to town, culminating in his movement from death to life. The apostles, anointed with the flickering flames and whispering wind of the Holy Spirit, spread into the entire world, baptizing and teaching in the name of God. Paul inherited his faith in a life-moving conversion experience during his wrong-headed road trip to Damascus, and for years did not stop traveling. Dorcas and Lydia moved among their peers to cement this new faith into a foundation for newly converted believers. And at the end of the testaments, this final movement-seeking plea was voiced on behalf of all God's people: "Even so, Lord, come quickly."

Movement in Spiritual Speech

Spiritual wisdom can find voice in expressions of movement. These few might jump-start the idea-generating activities of your mind:

- "Ask, and you will receive (mouth and throat system). Search, and you will find (leg and foot system). Knock and the door will be opened for you" (arm and hand system) (Matthew 7:7 CEV).
- The purposes of the church are expressed in God's great, moving commands: "You must love one another" (John 13:34 CEV) and "Go to the people of all nations and make them my disciples" (Matthew 28:19 CEV).
- The Christian life is a journey. As a pilgrim or sojourner, you are summoned away from a sedentary existence to accept God's invitation to move on, move forward, move into a life that fulfills God's will.
- One of the enduring images of God is "Yaweh," or "I am with you." Your God walks alongside as guide, friend, companion. God moves into your life and stays with you all the way.

- Disciples fill the footsteps of their Teacher, following where he has just recently walked and teaching what he first taught them.
- Your life moves because God first moved—creating, loving, forgiving, preserving—especially in the life and person of Jesus Christ, God's Son. Your life has purpose and meaning—implicitly moving words—because you have been moved by God's grace from sin to salvation to sanctified living.

Movement in Your Congregation

Your congregation is also called the body of Christ, and it depends on movement for its life. Your congregation could be named as a community of the moved and moving. See how these motion metaphors might depict your congregation:

- The seemingly chaotic scurryings and busyness of congregations at festival times may be like the atoms in your brain, adding a vitality to your congregation's identity.
- The mouth and throat movement system of your congregation gathers people into fellowship with Christ and God's people (witnessing).
- Your congregation's arm and hand system grasps and holds these individuals dearly, greeting and holding them in deeply satisfying relationships (fellowship).
- Gifted by the Word and Sacrament ministry (worship), your congregation enters the world as the leg and foot system of God's love, serving others as members of Christ's body and brain (ministry in daily life).
- Movement—of all your senses—is integral to the rituals and spirit of worship. Your eyes are drawn upward to symbols of faith embedded in your church's architecture or furnishings. Processionals and recessionals announce the beginnings and endings of these moments you set aside for God-encounters. The percussive and melodic music of worship invites your toes to tap, your energies to rise, your emotions to spill over. Prayers call forth the flow of tears.

The word of God—preached, sung, or prayed—compels you to reflection, and then action. The Spirit moves invisibly, like a warm spring breeze, and fills worshipers with assurance and courage for life's work. The work of worship is moving.

- Packets of spiritual energy move through the neuronal pathways of your congregation's brain. Good news—health, childbirth, blessed deaths, new beginnings—courses through your congregation's maze of interconnected affinities. Fearsome facts travel similar pathways, only more quickly, and fight, flight, and freeze suddenly appear as the best choices to protect you from danger.
- Individual members—like individual neurons—migrate toward the places where they are most needed. They take on new tasks and learn new skills. Thus your congregation's brain constantly repatterns itself for new ministry, new relationships.
- When your congregation stops moving—stops being concerned for others, stops seeking new stimuli, stops paying attention to already existing stimuli, stops changing—it dies. As surely as a brain with no synapses stops working, so too a congregation will die if the individual relationships among its members are not filled with the energy of trust and love.
- Your brain goes to church and meets God in the company of the larger brain of all of God's people. Then your church goes to the brain, as you meld your individual identities into God's will for your life together.

A Final Moving Word

To stay alive, your brain and your congregation move constantly. As you look at the ways you lead, consider how you can make movement important to everything you do. Think of yourself as a motion coach, or as an irresistible force undeterred by immovable objects because you are powered by God's gracious love and the Spirit's gifts. Think of yourself as a mover and shaker for God's purposes.

Move on!

Chapter 6

Your Brain Goes to Church
Coming and Going

BEFORE YOU PUT DOWN this book and get back to work, I'd like to share some final thoughts with you about your brain's coming and going. Then a thank you and a bless you. After a parting word, you're free to leave.

Coming

When you showed up at the start of this book, you and I exchanged promises: "I'll read this book, Bob, if you fill it with something important." You came to the book, with your brain eager to find out more about itself. You were ready to be mindful about your mind. I was mindful about your hope to find in this book something valuable for your congregational leadership.

Mindful is how I hope you come to the tasks and activities in which you engage as a congregational leader. Whether you're a pastor or a lay leader, I hope you show up at your leadership post with a brain fully engaged, a brain aware of its surroundings, its emotions, its capacities, its memories, and its wondrous qualities. I hope that your church-leader equipment includes a brain appreciative of the brains of other leaders, a brain motivated to work with them and energized by the possibilities ahead of you.

As you come to any activity or task in your congregation, keep in mind what you've read here. Recall the places I've told you about the pitfalls and bramble patches that can detract from your brain's choices for purposeful living. Determine how you can replace fear with love, heighten generosity, and gather wisdom for action. Combine some of what you've read into an informal evaluation tool by which to measure deeper aspects of effective leadership. Come to your vocation as a leader deeply respectful of God's wisdom in giving you your particular brain.

Whenever you're about to begin an activity or undertake any task in your congregation, take just a moment to consider the following questions:

- What's the state of my brain at this moment? How do I know?
- What will be required of my brain in the upcoming tasks or roles?
- What capabilities are already available in my brain? What capabilities will I need from the brains of others?
- What will I pray about?

When you're coming to your work as a church leader, always remember this truth: God has been here before you, will be here now, and will stay around long after you and your brain leave. Your brain is never alone.

Going

In scant minutes, your brain will instruct its visual input receptors to disengage from observing and processing these word-stimuli, your brain's motor cells will act in concert to shut the back cover, and your brain's long-term memory will complete its shifting and sorting in order to store what's useful or important for future reference. You'll be leaving, but your brain will take this book with you.

I hope that you can take this book with you into your leadership, that its premises make sense long after you are finished reading my sometimes logical and sometimes whimsical rhetoric. I hope that some fact, some question, some irksome proposition will needle you into taking a different course of action, seeing something a little differently, adding hope and energy where only despair and inactivity may have resided before.

Comings Are Goings Are Comings

The difference between an exit and an entrance is the direction you're facing. Look in and you're entering; look out and you're exiting. You came into this book—an entrance into brain science and congregations—hoping to come away from what may have been holding you back. Now you're at the end of this entrance, and it's looking like an exit—some small part of you is wondering if you could just stay here a bit longer.

But this book is also an entrance, a set of windows and doors to other places, other ideas about your brain and your congregation. I've taken you to those openings several times and now it's time for you to close the book and explore the places you've seen or imagined. Let me offer these few suggestions for your next set of comings and goings:

- Starting with the Web, start searching for trustworthy sources for current brain science information, with some implications for practice. Start with Brain Connection (http://www.brainconnection. com), a delightful, easy-to-understand collection of brain research, especially applied to learning.
- If you want my recommendations for up-to-date resources, try almost any major news magazine. With genetics, brain science is at the forward edge of our culture's continuing development. Two magazines I'd recommend are *Discover* and *Scientific American*. Both are written so that a science layperson can easily navigate the implications of fascinating new discoveries.
- Look for the next, even-better book about brain science and the church. Somewhere one is being researched and written right now. When it arrives at your neighborhood bookstore, give it a look and see what's new and useful. Perhaps you'll write the book.
- Require brain-based answers to your questions about procedural and structural changes in your congregation. It's not enough any-

more to rely on ecclesiastical pronouncements, philosophical truths, or sociological maxims in order to find out how you might become an effective leader.

- Talk to some educators about how brain-oriented ideas have helped change the shape and direction of education. (For example, educators now routinely help children and youth think about their thinking—mindfulness—and understand how students can direct their emotions positively.) See what applies to your congregation's life.
- Don't let anyone mess with your brain. Because attention is the prime commodity in today's world, there are plenty of folks who desperately want your attention, or who want to keep you afraid, angry, or compliant. Most likely they don't have your best interests in their brains. And for heaven's sake, watch out for the hucksters, whoever they might be; they're probably using brain-based techniques to persuade, dissuade, or assuage you.
- Enjoy your brain. You heard me right; have fun with your brain. For the sheer joy of it, watch yourself doing some routine task, and imagine all the millions of cells working together. Just for fun, work a word puzzle and think of the left and right hemispheres scrambling to find the right words and the right memories and connect them together with your visual capabilities and your motor neurons. Sometime, when you're praying, allow yourself to sink deeply into God's presence, asking God to fill your brain with what's good and right and beautiful. Laugh with God about the silly notion that, even with this marvelous brain, you could ever think of yourself as a minor deity come to Earth.
- Keep thanking God for your brain. Without turning into an amateur brain scientist, you can readily find good reasons every day that your brain works the way it does. Be specific, not for God's benefit (God already knows who you are and how God made you!), but for your own.

Thank You and Bless You

Thanks for paying attention to what you've read here; for starting to noodle about what these ideas might mean for you. This wasn't always easy, was it? Big words, big concepts, "what-ifs" that could have made your head hurt from all the thinking. But you stuck with it. Thanks. You've taken to heart some bits and pieces of this book, and put them to good use. Thanks again.

The blessing comes in a short-and-simple form: Gesundheit! Sneezer or nonsneezer, you deserve my "Be healthy!" blessing. Sneezer or nonsneezer—I always try my bad puns twice—you want to sustain the health and vitality of your congregation, to inspire and love the people you serve. By God's grace you're a blessing to others, so I offer my blessing to you—for your spirit and for your work as a leader.

A Final Word

The propositions that fill this book—about your brain and your congregation-as-brain—are interrelated. It's difficult to find words to express the full sense of how your brain works within itself, with your body and with your environment to make sense of and interact with all that you encounter. Perhaps the phrase that best characterizes the interrelationships of your brain with all that exists is a phrase usually ascribed to the church's identity and relationship with God: a mystical, sweet communion.

- **Mystical.** Finally, the best answers to "What is this brain?" are words of ineffability, comparatively tiny verbal pokings at something totally beyond knowing. *Exquisite* and *mysterious* come close to being adequate synonymns.
- **Sweet.** You can find great delight in the proposition that your brain is indescribably, deliciously wonderful. Its parts and structures and pieces work well with each other, despite your knowing how and why. Like a new automobile whose amazing features you keep discovering as you take it through its paces, your brain offers you more than you ask, with new possibilities and new surprises almost every day. Your brain connects together your self-awareness with your capacity for action so that you can accomplish God's mission for your life. What a pleasure to know that you don't have to be in charge

of the intricate connectivity that occurs within your brain at every moment. How incredibly fortunate that the whole of your brain is always greater than the sum of its parts.

- **Communion.** Your brain connects with itself and all that exists in the great cosmos of life. Your brain is formed from atoms that have existed throughout time, and so you are joined to the eons of God's eternal existence, to the billions of other brains that have ever existed. Your brain's living tissue affects the brains of countless other living things—in the environment, among your relationships, in the effects of your life on the rest of the people of the world. When the molecules of your brain cease to function as a unitary whole, they will reconstitute themselves eventually into some other, newer part of the created world. You are joined, living and lively, to God's purposes and God's creation for all of time. You're part of a congregation of people who believe the same. What a privilege.

Now, close this book and take that brain of yours to church. You have God's work to do.

Glossary

The words and definitions listed here provide a handy reference as you read this book. The definitions come to you in detail so that you will find new information even in these last pages. For further clarity about brain anatomy, I recommend the Web site, http://braininfo.rprc. washington.edu or the book, *How to Explain a Brain: An Educator's Handbook of Brain Terms and Cognitive Processes,* by Dr. Robert Sylwester (Thousand Oaks, Calif.: Corwin Press, Inc., 2004).

absolute unitary being (AUB). In neurotheology, a state of "pure mind" in which a brain is both super-quieted and also hyper-aware. In deep meditation and prayer, this state of being yields a feeling of ultimate union with God, other people, and all that exists.

affiliative neurocircuitry. Another way of talking about "the social brain," denoting how its functions are spread throughout your brain, functions likely hardwired into your brain as a default capability for pleasurable social interaction.

altruism. A feature of the "social brain." In sociology and psychology, the concern for others that may even transcend one's concern for self. The debate continues whether your brain enables this behavior for its own welfare only, or whether truly selfless acts are possible. Reciprocal altruism presumes that you undertake seemingly selfless acts because of the probability that others will return your regard.

amygdala. Paired almond-shaped structures located in the middle of your brain. A primary component of your limbic system, the amygdala consists of about a dozen clusters of neurons with varying functions. Each of these nodules is connected to other brain regions, sending and receiving signals that are central to the brain's emotional processing, especially fear. The amygdala is involved in regulating hormonal, autonomic, and motor functions of your brain, as well as reproduction, memory, sleep, facial recognition, and spatial orientation. The amygdala is especially tuned to investigate social ambiguity. For these reasons, it would be accurate to characterize the amygdala as a key component of your brain's social abilities.

anterior cingulate gyrus. Located at the top front of your brain (above your nose), the anterior cingulate gyrus processes decision-making in ambiguous situations (when several effective responses are possible). This small structure is a prime coordinator of attention, memory, somatic, and autonomic motor responses, motivation, and responses to pain. The cingulate has the ability to regulate its own levels of dopamine, and has extensive connections to many regions of your brain.

apoptosis. From a Greek word that names how a tree loses its leaves. Apoptosis is similar to *cell suicide,* the purposeful process by which your brain prunes unused or underutilized neurons so that the remaining cells have space and nutrients in which to operate efficiently.

a priori **assumptions.** The basic presumptions that form the foundation of any system of thought. In philosophy or theology especially, these postulates are made before (or are not subject to) examination or factual study. *A priori* assumptions are necessarily held to be true without question. An example from theology: "God exists." An example from philosophy: "I think, therefore I exist." A too-frequent example from church life: "This congregation is the pastor's responsibility."

autonomic system. Your brain's complex collection of structures that automatically regulate your body's vital functions. Divided into two subsystems, the autonomic nervous system includes the sympathetic system (which helps you prepare for fight/flight/freeze responses to stress or danger) and the parasympathetic system (which quiets your brain in order to allow more objective evaluation of information). The two subsystems work in a delicate tension, each contributing to the other's functioning. In your congregation, the autonomic system might be those individuals who are always available in an emergency (sympathetic system) and those who just keep plugging along quietly (parasympathetic system).

axon. The sending part of a neuron, the axon passes on information across a synapse to the dendrites of other neurons. A neuron typically has only one axon, which can extend to some length, and as many as 100,000 dendrites. (Might an axon in your congregation be individual members who can influence many other members?)

basal ganglia. A cluster of structures beneath the cortex that collaborate with the motor cortex and cerebellum to regulate voluntary movements. Parkinson's disease negatively affects basal ganglia functioning.

brainstem. About the size of a finger, your brainstem is located at the top of the spinal cord at the back of your brain. Its functions are mostly automatic, including maintaining your brain's general state of arousal. It regulates life support functions such as respiration and blood pressure. The brainstem helps you express emotions such as crying and laughing.

cell migration. By the eighth week of gestation, fetal neurons (stem cells or neuroblasts) migrate (grow or move) into the areas where they will eventually mature into organized groups of brain cells with varying functions. The neurons in the fetus are "social" from their start, joining together with other neurons to form connections, structures, and systems. In adult brains damaged or limited by disease or stroke, neurons can migrate into unused areas of the brain, taking up new or continuing functions. Cell migration is thus both a part of original cell generation and of cell regeneration.

cell pruning. Another way to talk about programmed cell death, especially notable in the last month of fetal development. Pruning is the elimination of weaker or nonfunctioning neurons for the overall benefit of the developing brain.

cell regeneration. Recent research suggests that throughout life your brain continues to exercise its capacity for regenerating neurons.

"Vacated synapses" can be reennervated by the nerve fibers left undamaged by cell death. Existing neurons can then migrate into brain areas left empty by the destruction of other neurons.

cerebellum. This "little brain"—the bump at the back of your brain—is connected to the brainstem, and is important for motor functions such as balance and coordination. The cerebellum also helps your brain focus attention. It stores your primitive physical reactions and the learned reactions that have become automatic. The physical proximity of the cerebellum and the limbic system may explain why movement and emotion each affect the other.

cerebrum. A term that is used to refer to the left and right cerebral hemispheres together. In some usage, *cerebrum* denotes a composite structure consisting of the cerebral cortex and the underlying cerebral white matter (the axons that connect neuronal networks). Sometimes *cerebrum* is a shorthand way to talk about the entire top sections of the brain.

chaos. In common use you might hear *mess* when this word or its derivatives are used. In developing theories about the composition of the physical world—primarily from complexity theory or quantum physics—*chaos* is a technical term that expresses the randomness of a collection of objects, processes, or physical properties. Another way to think of chaos: God's first creation was a world "without form and void" (Gen. 1:2 KJV). For complexity/chaos theorists, chaos—like order—is a temporary state of affairs, if only because order is not evident or has not yet emerged. In brain science, *chaos* accurately names what we cannot yet understand about the sometimes seemingly random activity of neuronal firings.

congregational brain. In this book, you'll see this term, as well as *congregation as brain,* used to compare your personal brain and the workings of the congregation as an organic whole. For the most part, the metaphor can serve you well as you try to understand how your congregation behaves in ways similar to each of the individual brains that comprise it.

corpus callosum. A bundle of about 200 million neuronal fibers connecting the left and right hemispheres of your brain. In the early days of brain science, deductions about the functions of your brain were made by examining the effects of surgeries that severed the corpus callosum. The two cerebral hemispheres seemed to process information in distinct ways, yielding the conclusion that the hemispheres were organized in separate but equal functions. When brain-imaging technologies emerged recently, the conclusions about specific hemispheric capabilities were considerably softened as scientists began to understand how interdependently the two hemispheres operate, while still retaining some specific functions.

cortex. The cortex is the part of your brain that processes conscious thoughts. The word comes from a Latin word that means "bark," because the cortex (or cerebral cortex) is a large, deeply folded sheet of neuronal tissue located just under your skull. The cortex consists of four large brain-paired structures called lobes (or divisions), one of each in each hemisphere. The sensory lobes are located towards the back of your brain, processing and interpreting incoming information. They are the occipital (back of the brain: vision), parietal (top of the brain: touch) and temporal (below the parietal lobes and above your ears: hearing). The frontal lobes (from about the ears forward) process decisions about how to respond to information sent forward from the sensory lobes.

cortisol. Your brain's "stress hormone," cortisol increases its levels in the brain under stressful or fearful situations, so that your body's defense mechanisms can go into action. Under the influence of high or continuing stress, however, cortisol levels increase to essentially toxic levels, increasing the metabolism of neurons so that they overheat and die.

dendrites. The branches on a neuron cell body, responsible for receiving information (across synapse gaps) from the axons of other neurons. If the axons on a brain cell "teach," then the dendrites "learn."

dopamine. Called the "learning neurotransmitter" because of its involvement with your brain's attention and reward systems, dopamine has several functions in your brain. Dopamine helps regulate your appetite, control muscle movement, place emotional tags on information, and strengthen or weaken memory. With endorphins, dopamine helps create your feelings of pleasure and joy. Those who suffer from Parkinson's disease have low concentrations of dopamine in their brain. Individuals who are diagnosed as ADHD (attention deficit hyperactivity disorder) may have high levels of dopamine.

Ebenezer stone. During the time of their seemingly endless battles with the resident Philistines, the Israelites fought and won an important battle at Mizpeh with the help of a horrifying thunderstorm. To commemorate this victory by God's own hand, Samuel set up a large stone monument that he called Ebenezer, which means "stone of help."

ecclesiology. In strict usage, the study of church art or architecture, but more broadly used to denote the study of the church as an institution. In current usage, *sociology of religion* may be a more accurate term. (Still, *ecclesiology* has a nice Greco-Latinate ring to it that just makes you want to say it out loud!)

emotional intelligence. Coined by Yale psychologist Peter Salovey in the 1990s and made popular in the work of science writer and psychologist Daniel Goleman, the term has come to depict a variety of personal intelligences in five major domains. They are: knowing one's emotions, managing emotions, motivating oneself, recognizing emotions in others, and handling relationships.

emotional neutrality. A fascinating new piece of social theory, emotional neutrality expresses the emotional—and perhaps moral—emptiness that develops in brains consistently overloaded with too much information. The basic science: the speed of information processing in the brain remains constant even while speeds of information intake can increase. The unprocessed information gets sloughed off—forgotten or not paid attention to—and hence the brain reacts to increasing information after only minimal integration of the information to emotional tagging mechanisms of the amygdala.

endorphins. Neurotransmitters that block pain and increase pleasure (or perhaps more accurately: comfort and well-being). From as early as 1975, scientists have known that morphine-based drugs are similar in chemical structure—and effects—to endorphins.

excitotoxicity. A complex cause of widespread neuronal death, implicated in strokes, epilepsy, and perhaps Alzheimer's disease. Excitotoxicity occurs when too much glutamate—normally a basic and necessary amino acid that excites neurons into firing—is present in the brain. An excess of calcium or oxygen may be connected with excess glutamate.

face recognition. A nearly mystical capability of your brain, especially the amygdala, to discern the meaning of literally hundreds of minute changes in the human face. A key feature of social intelligence, face recognition is acquired early in life, and persists as a remarkable and dependable skill throughout life. Face recognition may lie at the heart of mimicry, a primary form of learning.

false memories. Memories of events that are not factual. In false memories, your brain's memory-making mechanisms seem to work normally, but are actually heavily influenced by the persuasive suggestions of others. In the mid-1980s through the early 1990s there was an explosion of "recovered memory" incidents involving supposedly scandalous conduct by childcare operators, parents, and other care providers. Many turned out to be false memories.

glial cells. A system of a trillion brain cells—separate from the 100 billion neurons in the human brain. The main functions of glial cells have until recently been seen primarily as protecting and maintaining neuronal health. Recently, evidence has emerged that the glial cells may have other important functions in the brain. Glial cells seem to communicate with each other primarily via chemical signals.

glucose. Your brain uses glucose—sugar water—as its primary nutrient, but has no storage facility for glucose. Without replenishment, your current supply of glucose can be depleted within 5 to 10 minutes. About 25 percent of the glucose your body ingests is used by your brain.

glutamate. The amino acid glutamate is also a major excitatory neurotransmitter (one that stimulates neurons to fire). It is found throughout your brain, perhaps in half the neurons. Glutamate in your congregation might be regular worship or prayer.

gnosticism. A continuing heresy within Christianity that holds body and soul to be distinct from the other, attributing positive attributes to the soul and negative attributes to the body. Early gnostics debated the divinity and humanity of Christ. Contemporary gnostics might have trouble with brain science findings about the integration of mind and body.

God's Word/word. In its uppercase manifestations, a term that denotes Christ; in its lowercase form, *word* indicates the revelation of God in the Bible. The embodiment of God's word in God's Word shows God's nature and God's will for those who want to serve God with body, mind, and soul.

growth hormone. A necessary hormone for normal brain development, growth hormone is regulated by the hypothamalus—your brain's "control center." Its availability to your brain can be affected by trauma, diet, stress, or social support.

gyrus. The outside of your brain looks like a wadded-up dinner napkin (and it's about that size). An external ridge in the deeply folded cerebral cortex is called a *gyrus* (for example, the anterior cingulate gyrus), and an indentation or furrow is called a *sulcus* (such as the central sulcus that separates the frontal and sensory hemispheric lobes).

habituation. Your brain's ability to turn repeated brain functions or responses into "default" actions, thus saving your brain the work of constantly attending to all incoming stimuli and making coordinated decisions regarding them. Habituation might be another way to think about automatic memories.

hardwiring. The neuronal connections you inherit genetically, expressed by the time you are born. In some popular usage, the term also characterizes any behavior that becomes habituated or automatic. Sometimes used as a proof for deterministic views of human nature. (As in "I'm hardwired to be self-centered, so I'll just give in and become selfish.")

hermeneutic. In philosophy, the rules (or forms) in which arguments and persuasion take place. In theology, the rules and methods by which Scripture is interpreted.

hippocampus. A seahorse-shaped structure in the inner parts of your brain that is strongly implicated in the formation and retrieval of long-term declarative (or factual) memories. *Hippocampus* is the Greek word for "seahorse," which might give you a clue about how some brain structures got their names!

hypothalamus. About the size of a cherry, the hypothalamus is located at the very center of your brain, a convenient and necessary location for its functions in coordinating just about every brain function. For example, the hypothalamus is involved in sexual arousal, the secretion of hormones, fight/flight/freeze responses, sleep, hunger and thirst, blood circulation, and body temperature.

intelligent design. The quasi-scientific theory that we can infer the existence and work of an intelligent Creator God from the design— beauty, intricacy, complexity—of creation, including the human brain. As old as early church theologians Ireneaus and Origen, these arguments have recently come into favor again—especially in the fields of biology and cosmology—as the most logical explanations for the origin of the universe and the development of Homo sapiens, the supposedly "intelligent" species.

intralaminar nuclei. Neurons deep inside the thalamus. By some accounts, the most likely biological explanation of *consciousness*. Their extra-long axons connect many areas of the brain, allowing your brain to maintain a background hum of 40 hertz throughout all of its structures. The brain is thus unified and able to undertake other functions, much like how instruments in an orchestra each have their separate functions but play to the same beat.

limbic system. A term coined by Dr. Paul MacLean in the 1950s. Although it is not currently as widely accepted as useful or accurate, the term *limbic system* groups together an ill-defined ring of interconnected cortical and subcortical structures surrounding the brainstem. The limbic system has long been considered the central location for emotional activity and memory. In common use, the structures of this system include the amygdala, hippocampus, hypothalamus, fornix, cingulate, and septum. *Limbic* (Latinate term for "border") is used to name these structures because they border the inner surface of the temporal lobes.

long-term memory. The large store of memory that remains reliable over an extended period of time. Dependent on the initial work of short-term (working) memory, long-term memory is a function of various brain structures, especially the hippocampus. Dreaming (during REM sleep) may be the way your brain consolidates and organizes long-term memories for future use.

long-term potentiation (LTP). After firing patterns are established through repetition, neurons are potentially more likely to seek and continue that arrangement into the future. LTP denotes changes in the synaptic chemistry of individual neurons and groups of neurons. LTP could explain how a single cell "learns" and "remembers." In your congregation, LTP might show up as your first or most frequently chosen responses to familiar situations.

mammalian brain. The middle part of Paul MacLean's *triune brain,* located above the brainstem and below the cortex. The mammalian brain loosely describes limbic areas of your brain that are engaged in the struggle for survival, including coordinated movement, memory, emotion, and primitive social intelligence. Also called the *paleomammalian brain.*

materialism. In brain science, the word refers to a theory about brain functioning that reduces the intricate relationships and operations of the brain to the most basic actions of individual neurons or chemicals. Thus the term is a close synonym to *reductionism* in other areas of biology. Not related to *materialism* in social science and theology, in which the term connotes our overdependence on material goods or physical comfort for our sense of well-being.

metaphysics. At the junction where quantum physics, philosophy, and theology meet, metaphysics attempts to explain first causes and problems of ultimate reality. Includes the study of being (ontology) and the study of the structure of the universe (cosmology). Metaphysicians are exploring brain science because its theorems and discoveries may explain some of life's ultimate complexities. The term means "after physics" because Aristotle's treatise on transcendental philosophy followed his work on physics.

mindfulness. A useful way to describe "full attention," or the shifting of your brain's awareness from background to foreground. In learning theories and social science, mindfulness is sometimes a synonym for "whole brain learning" or altruism.

motor cortex. A narrow band of brain tissue that extends over your brain from ear to ear. It initiates and coordinates intentioned physical movement—of eyes, hands, arms, legs, torso, tongue, etc.—toward desired results. The brain circuits that order, sequence, and time a mental act are the same ones used to order, sequence, and time a physical act.

myelin. The fatty substance that covers neurons much like the insulation on wires. (Sometimes called *myelin sheath*.) Myelin emerges out of glial cells, and helps neurons transmit information efficiently. A simple way to understand the function of myelin: the better the insulation, the less electrical energy can dissipate from the wire. Multiple sclerosis is an illness that results from the breakdown of myelin, thus short-circuiting movements.

neocortex. Another term for *cortex,* but laden with evolutionary explanations: "The cortex of the human brain arrived late in the overall development of Homo sapiens."

neuro. A lingual prefix easily attached to a variety of nouns, verbs, and adjectives. (See following entries.) This important function of language will likely allow for future terms such as *neuroexegetics, neurosermon* or *neuroboring*. A linguistic relative of "brain-based." In the future, both "neuro" and "brain-based" will likely continue to be overused and overapplied.

neuroblasts. In the fetus, neural stem cells that migrate to the areas of the brain where they will mature into full-fledged neurons. Recent evidence indicates that neuroblasts may remain active into adulthood, useful in the regeneration of brain cells later in life.

neuroeconomics. A curious new example of applied brain science, in this case the blending of neurobiology and economics. One recent neuroeconomical question that may soon find its way into a legal challenge: Who has the economic rights to "attention," especially if *your* especially persuasive advertising infringes on *my* desire to ignore your product? (Perhaps "financial generosity" or "contributions" may become a subset of this barely formed variant of biology and economics.)

neuron. One kind of basic brain cell, consisting of a single (signal sending) axon, the cell body and as many as 100,000 (signal receiving) dendrites. Your brain contains a jungle of about 100 billion neurons. (See **glial cells** for a description of another type of brain cells that exists in far greater abundance than neurons.)

neuroplasticity. The ability of neurons to change their physical state and function in response to changes in their environment, making new connections with other neurons. In brief, the brain's ability to rewire itself.

neuroscience. A growing body of knowledge about the brain and nervous system, primarily focused on their biology. Hence also *neurobiology*. Necessarily dependent on "brain theory," proven and as-yet-unproven theses about the importance of scientific discoveries about the brain. Not connected with *brain conjecture*, a growing body of unproven and unconnected musings about the meaning and importance of even the tiniest shred of evidence about the brain.

neurotheology. Recently coined, the term denotes the connection between brain science and theology. Dependent on both mystical and metaphysical elements of theology, this field of inquiry takes advantage of brain-imaging technology to observe physical changes in the brain as spiritual states of mind are experienced. An observation: Since self-idolatry persists as part of the human condition, neurotheology may falsely legitimate a religion in which the human brain is worshiped and glorified as preeminent reality.

neurotransmitter. Any one among scores of chemical compounds in your brain (and body) that enable chemical information to pass from one neuron to another at a synapse. Sometimes known by their chemical names—"endorphins" are the same as "endogenous opioid peptides." Human and animal neurotransmitters are very similar, allowing scientists to derive information from experiments with rats and monkeys. Among the most common neurotransmitters are dopamine, endorphins, oxytocin, and serotonin. Some body hormones also function as neurotransmitters as they occur in the brain.

nucleus accumbens. A small cluster of cells in the forebrain consistently identified as a major component of your brain's "pleasure center." Well connected to the limbic system, the nucleus accumbens contains one of your brain's highest concentrations of the neuro-transmitter dopamine. The nucleus accumbens is implicated in addiction mechanisms, and in your brain's attention sequencing.

olfactory bulb. A rudimentary protuberance in the human brain that mimics the much larger olfactory brain functions of other mammals and thus processes your sense of smell. A related system processes pheromones—molecules that help regulate sexual attraction and repulsion. Although the human sense of smell is not as powerful as that of most animals, it still plays a key role in many human behaviors, such as eating.

oscillation. Your entire brain "hums" or vibrates at a rate of 40 cycles per second (40 hertz). Like the steady, subtle purring of cars idling in a parking lot or the background rustling of a Sunday congregation preparing for worship, this "brain noise" is the background sound of your brain at rest.

oxytocin. An important hormone secreted by the pituitary gland that initiates uterine contractions in childbearing and lactation in breast-feeding. It also helps us to affiliate, bond, and nurture. Males and females have both oxytocin and vasopressin (see later entry), but oxytocin levels tend to be higher in females, and vaso-pressin levels tend to be higher in males. The hormones play an essential role in most positive human interactions. At times of stress, oxytocin may predispose women more towards tend/befriend responses than fight/flee/freeze responses.

panentheism. A system of theological thought—sometimes connected to process theology—in which the world and God are understood as related-yet-distinct realities. Theologians of this stripe are no doubt wrestling with the difficult questions of "the mind of God" and "Christ dwelling within us."

pantheism. An older—and more familiar—model of God, in which God and the world are collapsed into a single unified whole. In its aberrant forms, *pantheism* confuses the natural world (including the brain?) with God, thus allowing the worship of the natural world, including the brain. The theological problem here: your brain becomes your God, and you worship yourself.

parasympathetic nervous system. One part of your brain's autonomic (automatic) nervous system, the parasympathetic system quiets your brain for more objective evaluation of information. A "quieted brain" is made possible by a lower heart rate, slower rate of breathing, lower blood pressure—all functions of the parasympathetic nervous system. Another net result of this system's work: conserving of the body's store of energy.

prayer. From the viewpoint of neurotheology, one means by which absolute unitary being (AUB) is achieved in the human brain. (See the earlier entry on this subject.) From the viewpoint of theology, communication with God.

prefrontal cortex. The foremost part of your brain, right behind your forehead. Involved in working memory, guidance for the motor cortex, planning, deliberation, learning, depression, and other higher cognitive processing. Connected to every system in your brain, it is often called the brain's chief executive officer (CEO). Among its lesser-known functions: providing a place for head-scratching brought on by the reading of glossary entries about the brain.

programmed cell death. A fascinating feature of most organisms, this purposeful destruction of cells in your brain—enabling its overall efficiency—is an internally controlled process by which neurons suffer a breakdown in their viability. Another name for this phenomenon: *cell suicide.* An absence of neuronal growth factor (NGF) is the presenting cause for neurons to waste away, and "suicide genes" may be hardwired into your brain to initiate the process.

psycholinguistics. An offshoot of some early applications of brain science, in which the insights of psychology and linguistics were connected in order to explain the development of language—including the acquisition of literacy—and the effects of language on the human psyche. Among the most memorable psycholinguistic maxims this writer remembers: Words—their variety, their complexity, their volume—determine the ways in which we think; no words, no thought. Thus the question, "How will these words become thought patterns?" is as important as "How can I put these thoughts into words?"

reductionism. In its several varieties applied to brain science, the proposition that the brain is essentially a collection of neurons and chemical/electrical components. Thus the study of the smallest element of brain science—a synapse, for example—can be used as the basis for inferring larger and more complex constructs. Given the present state of neurobiological experiments—the ease by which single cell research can take place in comparison to whole functioning brain experiments—reductionistic ideas may be the best we can derive for now.

reptilian brain. The brainstem and surrounding structures in MacLean's *triune brain*. These brain areas are centers for regulating the most basic brain functions. Included in the reptilian brain's work: sleep and waking, respiration, temperature regulation, autonomic movement, and the fight/flee/freeze response to danger.

serotonin. A neurotransmitter implicated in seemingly every function of the brain. Among its known functions at the time of this writing: controlling aggression, inhibiting anger, providing feelings of pleasure, enhancing motivation, limiting fear and worry, increasing and maintaining sexual attraction and attachment, relieving depression, limiting insomnia, and increasing feelings of serenity and calm. Selective serotonin reuptake inhibitors (such as Prozac) help make more serotonin available when naturally occurring levels are low.

short-term memory. See **working memory.**

simul justus et peccator. The Latin phrase can be translated, "simultaneously (justified) saint and sinner." An important Reformation principle—especially for Martin Luther—by which the seemingly contradictory behaviors of human beings are held in philosophical and theological tension. *Simul justus et peccator* might also be biologically accurate, given the following: Paul MacLean's *triune brain* theory, the hardwiring of both socially harmful and socially beneficial behaviors and the seemingly contradictory effects of brain hormones such as testosterone and oxytocin.

social brain. A nearly metaphoric term that describes a collection of hardwired brain functions and chemicals that enable humans to interact positively with each other. Examples of the social brain at work: altruism, face recognition, bonding behavior, nurturing "instincts," love and intimacy, free will, empathy, social intelligence, and language.

sojourner. An important theological concept for early Judaism—and by extension, early Christianity as well. The sojourner values the journey as much as arriving at a destination; sojourning acknowledges that searching pilgrims are not attached to "here" and "now" permanently. A humble philosophical position, in which one acknowledges God's ownership of all that exists, and God's guidance in all that happens. From the viewpoint of brain science, an accurate description of the meaning-making and newness-seeking of the human brain. Sometimes paired with "the steward" to indicate the Christian's responsibility for both the journey and other sojourners.

substantia nigra. The part of your brain that produces dopamine and sends it to the striatum, a brain structure that coordinates movement. In Parkinson's disease, cell death in the *substantia nigra* results in decreasing supplies of dopamine, and the loss of coordinated movement. Implanted fetal stem cells can encourage the growth of new neurons in the substantia nigra. The substantia nigra also seems to be involved in your brain's "self-referencing," its ability to strengthen the connections between perceptions and responses, a crucial element in learning.

synapse. Both the place and moment where or when electrical energy—in the form of a neurotransmitter—passes from a neuron's sending axon to one or more receiving dendrites of other neurons. As "place," the synapse is a narrow gap between an axon and its receiving dendrite(s). As "moment," the synapse is the instant when an electrical signal is briefly changed into a chemical signal and then back again. Synapses are the foundation for the brain's activity. In congregational life, synapses might be equivalent to the gap between a pastor's mouth and the congregation's ears.

synaptic weakening. Occurs when the chemical receptors on either side of a synapse—on the axon or the dendrites—gradually stop receiving messages. Perhaps associated with a decrease in dopamine at the synapse, a condition connected with advancing age *in some individuals.*

testosterone. Like most hormones, testosterone is found in the bodies and brains of both men and women. (But men have more testosterone than women, just as women have more estrogen than men.) Higher testosterone levels in men seem to correlate with increased tendencies toward aggression, competition, assertiveness, and physical vigor. During stress, levels of testosterone increase in men, leading to the fight/flight/freeze response. In males, testosterone stimulates the production of another hormone, vasopressin. (See later entry.) In women, testosterone is associated with ovulation and increased sexual interest.

thalamus. A relatively large structure right in the middle of your brain. Its two lobes are a kind of "central relay station" that coordinates the movement of information to and from other parts of your brain for use by the cortex. Input from all of your senses—except, strangely enough, your sense of smell—passes through the thalamus. In stressful situations, the thalamus sends signals along a more rapid pathway—to the amygdala—so that quick assessment of possible danger can be made.

triune brain. First proposed by biologist Paul MacLean in 1967, this big picture view of the brain tells more about the development of the human brain over time than it details the brain's present functions and structures. In MacLean's theory, the "original" brain is the reptilian brain—so called because its shape resembles the brain of reptiles—which undertakes the brain's most basic tasks. (See **reptilian brain.**) The next level, above and surrounding the reptilian, is the mammalian brain, whose shape and functions resemble the brains of most mammals. (See **mammalian brain.**) The outer, much larger and more recent brain, in MacLean's view, is the neocortex, that portion of the brain responsible for "higher order thinking," including abstract thinking, planning, and responding to changing situations. Perhaps the most striking characteristic of MacLean's work is that for several decades it remained a viable construct for understanding the brain. More recently, the strength of the theory has diminished in the light of brain imaging discoveries.

vasopressin. A powerful hormone especially evident in men. The effects of this hormone in sexual behavior may include increasing sexual arousal, enhancing sexual attraction, and increasing territoriality and jealousy. Vasopressin and the chemically similar female hormone, oxytocin, are produced in the brain's pituitary gland. At times of stress, vasopressin levels in men increase remarkably, leading some researchers to the conjecture that the guarding and protecting behavior of men can be attributed to this hormone. Other positive attributes of vasopressin may include its role in pair bonding and social memory—who's friend and who's foe.

working memory. Also known as *short-term memory,* working memory is your brain's way of registering current activities while also activating long-term memory. "Memories of the future" are also a function of working memory, allowing you at one moment to predict what will happen in the next moment, based on what has just occurred.

Bibliography

Black, Ira. *The Dying of Enoch Wallace: Life, Death, and the Changing Brain.* New York: McGraw-Hill, 2001.

Carter, Rita. *Exploring Consciousness.* Berkeley, Calif.: University of California Press, 2002.

Dozier, Rush W., Jr. *Fear Itself: The Origin and Nature of the Powerful Emotion.* New York: St. Martin's Press, 1998.

Flaherty, Alice W. *The Midnight Disease: The Drive to Write, Writer's Block, and the Creative Brain.* Boston: Houghton Mifflin Company, 2004.

Gardner, Howard. *Intelligence Reframed: Multiple Intelligences for the 21st Century.* New York: Basic Books, 2000.

Goldberg, Elkhonon. *The Executive Brain: Frontal Lobes and the Civilized Mind.* London: Oxford University Press, 2001.

Goleman, Daniel. *Working with Emotional Intelligence.* New York: Bantam Doubleday Dell, 2000.

Hogue, David A. *Remembering the Future, Imagining the Past: Story, Ritual and the Human Brain.* Cleveland: The Pilgrim Press, 2003.

Jaworski, Joseph. *Synchronicity: The Inner Path of Leadership.* San Francisco: Berrett-Koehler, 1998.

Johnson, Steven. "Antonio Damasio's Theory of Thinking Faster and Faster." *Discover* 25, no. 5 (2004): 44–49.

———. *Mind Wide Open: Your Brain and the Neuroscience of Everday Life.* New York: Scribner, 2004.

Koestenbaum, Peter, and Peter Block. *Freedom and Accountability at Work: Applying Philosophic Insight to the Real World.* San Francisco: Jossey-Bass/Pfeiffer, 2001.

McCrone, John. *Going Inside: A Tour Round a Single Moment of Consciousness.* New York: Fromm International, 2001.

Newberg, Andrew, Eugene D'Aquili, and Vince Rause. *Why God Won't Go Away.* New York: Ballantine Books, 2001.

Peterson, Gregory. *Minding God: Theology and the Cognitive Sciences.* Minneapolis: Fortress Press, 2002.

Pinker, Steven. *The Blank Slate: The Modern Denial of Human Nature.* New York: Viking Penguin, 2002.

Ratey, John J. *A User's Guide to the Brain: Perception, Attention and the Four Theaters of the Brain.* New York: Pantheon, 2001.

Restak, Richard. *The New Brain: How the Modern Age Is Rewiring Your Mind.* Emmaus, Pa.: Rodale Press, 2003.

Rogers, Lesley. *Sexing the Brain.* New York: Columbia University Press, 2001.

Salzman, Mark. *Lying Awake.* New York: Vintage Books, 2001.

Schwarz, Jeffrey M., and Sharon Begley. *The Mind and the Brain.* New York: ReganBooks, 2002.

Sylwester, Robert. *A Biological Brain in a Cultural Classroom.* 2nd ed. Thousand Oaks, Calif.: Corwin Press, 2003.

Taylor, Shelley E. *The Tending Instinct.* New York: Times Books, 2002.

Zimmer, Carl. "Whose Life Would You Save?" *Discover* 25, no. 4 (2004): 60–65.

Index